NOT-FOR-PROFIT

NOT-FOR-PROFIT

Barry P. Keating
University of Notre Dame

Maryann O. Keating
Saint Mary's College

THOMAS HORTON AND DAUGHTERS
22 Appleton Place, Glen Ridge, New Jersey 07028

ISBN 0-913878-18-9

CONTENTS

ACKNOWLEDGEMENT

We are grateful, most of all, to Professors Gordon Tullock and James M. Buchanan of Virginia Polytechnic Institute and State University, who, although they are in no way responsible for the book, certainly parented the ideas and provides the inspiration.

In addition, we wish to acknowledge the forebearance and comments of students at Radford University, The University of Notre Dame, and St. Mary's College with whom we worked out the formulation and exposition. Special thanks are due to our colleagues Professors Rita Cassidy, John T. Croteau, and James Rakowski, who made valuable comments on parts of the manuscript.

Beatrice Recker typed and retyped the manuscript in addition to all her other duties at Notre Dame. Finally, we are pleased to have shared the development of the book with editors Tom and Ann Horton. Our friendship with them predates even the existence of our sons, John and Vincent, to whom this book is fondly dedicated.

PART I

NEITHER FOR
LOVE NOR PROFIT

1

INTRODUCTION

Not-For-Profit does not presume to know all the answers or even to raise all the questions involved with the not-for-profit firm; it is designed to provide the reader with two things: a philosophy by which one evaluates a not-for-profit firm exclusively in terms of how well it provides the intended good or service; an analysis of the structure and theory of operation, common to all not-for-profit firms.

There are two positions presented in this book. The first position concerns the institutional structure of a not-for-profit firm and the second concerns the legitimacy in questioning the effectiveness of the not-for-profit firm.

The structure of an organization to a large extent determines the outcome. Too often it is assumed that different types of people are drawn to different types of organizations. Proponents of this view suggest that greedy types are drawn to business; humanitarians, to public service. Or, depending on one's viewpoint, productive individuals go into business and lazy ones into not-for-profit firms. It is assumed throughout this book that individuals are similarly motivated and operate within an organization in a fashion consistent with the institution's constraints (read rewards and incentives). In other words, the greed and productivity observed in business or, on the other hand, the humanitarianism and inefficiency in not-for-profit firms are a reflection of the type of organization. Not-for-profit firms are different, and one cannot expect them to perform as profit-seeking ones, or vice versa for that matter.

The second major position presented in the book concerns the legitimacy in questioning the effectiveness of not-for-profit firms. The questions deal with the types of goods and services these firms produce, with the methods by which these goods are produced, and with the way in which the goods, once produced, are distributed. In addition, one may question if not-for-profit firms tend to produce too much or too little and if those who pay for the goods consume them.

It is sometimes thought that if employees or customers could reestablish the profit-seeking firm as a co-operative (see insert), the concern of these groups for the well being of the organization would increase effectiveness. This may or may not be true. The effectiveness of profit-seeking firms lies in the extent to which management, constrained by the charge of its owners to maximize their equity or return, can provide service to its customers; similarly, the effectiveness of a not-for profit firm depends on the extent to which the administration, constrained by the interest of the sponsors, can provide service to its clients. But it is not easy to do this in a not-for-profit firm; the client, the sponsor and the employee may all be the same; namely, John Q. Public. The interests of the groups, as groups, in the firm are clearly complex and in many cases overlapping.

The content of this study falls quite naturally into five rather well-defined parts, themselves subdivided into chapters dealing with identifiable elements. Part I explores the intricacies of the not-for-profit firm, public and private, and Part II deals with the motivations of and control by administrators who operate not-for-profit firms. How do these administrators differ from managers in profit-seeking firms? Do they have more or less freedom or power in exercising their responsibilities? Part III, describing the types of products and services produced by not-for-profit firms, is essentially an outline of the markets in which they operate. Part IV is concerned with production decisions and internal workings, with emphasis on the relationships among the administration, clients, staff, and sponsor of a particular firm. Part V looks at planning techniques (e.g. Planning, Programming and Budgeting and Linear Programming), and, recognizing the difficulties of measuring effectiveness, analyzes the selection of appropriate performance indicators. Finally, the book concludes with a discussion of alternatives designed to steer not-for-profit firms to greater effectiveness.

Between Fifteenth and Sixteenth Streets in Northwest Washington, D.C., near New Hampshire Avenue, stands the Northumberland, an apartment house, built in 1908. In 1920 the owners of the building sold the apartments to the occupants.

Since that time, a continuous system for the maintenance and care of the building has been followed. A board, which meets once a month, was established to make decisions. Prospective buyers must be approved by current residents. No pets or children are permitted; the first rule is overlooked but the second enforced. Monthly assessments are made and much of the maintenance is done cooperatively.

The Northumberland is the oldest continuous housing cooperative in Washington. Recently, however, not only in Washington, but particularly in Chicago and New York, occupants are buying out the owners of their apartments. In many cases, the owners are only too happy to sell, which should lead to some suspicion on the part of buyers! But, in any case, cooperatives or condominiums are only two among many variations of Not-For-Profit Firms.

2

CHARACTERIZING THE SPECIES — WHAT IS A NOT-FOR-PROFIT FIRM?

What do the Department of Defense and the Society for the Prevention of Cruelty to Animals have in common? Like many cooperatives, hospitals, schools, regulatory agencies, orchestras, health clinics, welfare systems, credit unions, research foundations and health insurance programs, they are not-for-profit firms.

Although the Department of Defense and the Society for the Prevention of Cruelty to Animals are not operated for profit, there is a basic difference between the two organizations. The Department of Defense, like state universities, welfare departments and community hospitals, is sponsored by some governmental organization. The government organization may be local, state, or federal. Henceforth, this type of firm will be referred to as a public not-for-profit firm.

The Society for the Prevention of Cruelty to Animals, the Northumberland, Harvard University, Blue Cross and Blue Shield, and the Unification Church are not sponsored by government organizations but by groups of (private) individuals. This type of firm will be referred to as a private not-for-profit firm.

The major differences between firms, however, are not between private and public firms, but rather between profit-making enterprises and not-for-profit ones. A student trained in business may view the organizational structure of governments or universities as chaotic. He or she may even consider any deviation from the ways a profit-seeking firm operates as an institutional flaw. Thus business managers have often tried to reorganize not-for-profit firms to be more like the organizations they understand...business firms. But this may be as futile as trying to get a cat to bark!

External Differences Between Profit-Seeking and Not-For-Profit Firms

Most large profit-making firms, with the exception of regulated monopolies, operate in a competitive product market. These firms produce numerous products for many customers and most customers can switch rather than fight. The customers may also delay their purchases or even produce the product themselves.

The only long-term source of financing for such a profit-making firm is from the sale of its products. It can borrow money or float commercial paper, but these sources of financing dry up rather quickly when a firm is losing money on its products. The rates of both new business formation and business failure are comparatively high. Witness the coming and going of boutiques and pizza shops in many neighborhoods.

Not-for-profit firms, in contrast, are more likely monopoly suppliers of services to a single market. There are many exceptions to the similarity with monopoly suppliers, particularly in the case of private not-for-profit firms. Church schools and credit unions compete in vigorous service markets, albeit with subsidies from their sponsors; but many large unions and health care plans operate without a great deal of competition.

In the case of a government bureau, the firm exchanges a commitment to supply services for a periodic budget. The government has the power to tax and is generally a monopoly supplier in a given area. For example, it is often the case that residents must buy water from the city producer. This is also true, of course, for national defense, police protection and highways. Many individuals argue that some government services like schools, libraries, and parks are not monopolies because individuals are free to select alternatives in the private market. True, but one is not free to avoid paying for them once they are provided publicly.

Public not-for-profit firms characteristically rely on specialized financial instruments not available to profit-seeking firms. These instruments include taxation, the right to print money and issue tax-free bonds, and, on occasion, conscription and expropriation.

Government organizations are not likely to become extinct. Herbert Kaufman in his book *Are Government Organizations Immortal?* notes that rates of both new bureau formation and of bureau failure are comparatively low. Once a government firm receives an appropriation, it is apt to be borne along by the budgetary process. However, competition among agencies may be very keen and changing circumstances may force the agency to redefine its purpose.

Internal Differences

Internal differences tend to be less important than external differences between profit-seeking firms and not-for-profit enterprises. The distinctive internal characteristic of a profit-seeking firm is to facilitate survival in a competitive market.

This is why it is ineffective to transplant characteristics of profit-seeking firms on not-for-profit firms in the name of efficiency, unless external competitive conditions are changed.

There are some internal differences which are interesting and probably significant. Profit seeking firms, for example, place substantially greater reliance on financial rewards and employment sanctions. A substantial proportion of the income of higher managers is a residual claim in the form of a bonus or stock option based on the firm's earnings or stock performance. There are few analogies to this type of financial reward in most not-for-profit firms.

In general the ratio of salary to non-salary (employee benefits) is much higher in profit-seeking firms and would probably be even higher if income tax rates were lower. In addition, managers in profit-seeking enterprises are more easily fired for poor performance and workers more easily laid off due to declining demand.

Accounting is different in the two types of enterprises. Accounts in profit-seeking firms include both a balance sheet and an accrual-based income statement. Few governments or bureaus ever draw up a balance sheet and no decisions are made on balance sheet considerations, that is, on the basis of net worth. Government and bureau budgets are usually cash flow statements, because capital expenditures are budgeted at the time of purchase and never again.

In the profit-seeking sector, it is easier to gain approval for a new capital expenditure when the expected returns are high, and it is harder to hoard capital in an activity when the expected returns are low. New government or not-for-profit activities, on the other hand, are likely to be capital-starved and older activities are likely to capital-rich. In other words, a firm would tend to switch capital from a top-of-the-line product to a bottom-of-the-line product, if more money could be made by doing so. A local government, on the other hand, will be slower to switch capital from schools to hospitals, for example, even if most of the population are senior citizens quite beyond their child-bearing years!

Similarities

What surprises many is how similar are the internal organization incentives and procedures of profit-seeking and not-for-profit enterprises. A government official from the Pentagon or the Soviet Union without any specialized knowledge of production processes or the product market would perform well in most middle management positions. The immediate incentive for managers in both situations is identical. Please your superior, and, if your superior is in trouble or you have a difficult relationship with him or her, try to establish a good relationship with his or her superior.

The sociology of both types of firms is similar. People play the same games. The games include who has the best or biggest office, who answers the phone, who sits where at a meeting, who merely looks busy, who to see socially, etc.

It is not difficult to understand why many individuals conclude that large organizations, profit or not-for-profit, are basically alike. They are not. However, the basic problem of any organization, profit-seeking or not-for-profit, is the same: how to translate incentives of senior managers into the operationally identical incentives offered to lower level managers. In a profit-seeking enterprise, this problem is helped by the combination of financial incentives and the business accounting conventions.

In both public and private not-for-profit institutions, administrators of major divisions have surprisingly little discretion on capital spending and staffing. Administrators are expected to minimize the costs of meeting a given production schedule. However, the ratio of capital to labor may be determined or approved by higher managers. In other words, administrators are expected to be managers, not entrepreneurs. In addition, administrators usually need the approval of the next higher-level manager for the most routine requisition.

The practice of assigning tasks to lower-level managers is identical in large not-for-profit firms and private profit-seeking corporations. The results are also the same. A manager of a component that is already very efficient in terms of the task will have trouble handling an emergency. But a manager that has programmed in some slack or excess capacity may be able to exceed his task or meet an emergency situation. This tendency to build in slack is offensive to efficiency lovers in both the public and private sectors. Managers can be permitted to ask for and receive exemptions, but most managers will try to build in some slack to meet the next case because he or she cannot afford to ask for exemptions on a regular basis.

The point to be made is that there are great differences between the environments of profit-seeking and not-for-profit firms. Therefore, it is inappropriate to try to force not-for-profit firms to change their internal structures to be more businesslike. To do so will not necessarily increase efficiency.

On the other hand, there are great similarities between the two types of firms, particularly internally. The problems of incentives, control and task assignment, for example, are identical. The main differences concern the type of market in which the two institutions deal, particularly with respect to funding. These differences are responsible for the distinctive internal accommodation that we note in the not-for-profit firm.

3

THE PROPAGATION OF THE

NOT-FOR-PROFIT FIRM

There are three major sectors of the economy. The profit sector that sells a product for a price, the public sector that has the power to tax, and the private not-for-profit sector sometimes called the voluntary nonprofit sector. Most suspect that the public (i.e. government) sector is becoming a larger part of the economy. By precisely how much is not clear. The goal of this chapter is to define the size of the public and private not-for-profit sectors.

The Size and Growth of the Public Sector

There is no single index showing the growing economic importance of government activity. To indicate how particular aspects of government activity can be measured, data on gross national product, taxes and transfer payments, and government employment are presented.

The growth of government purchases of goods and services (Table 3-1) as recorded in the national income accounts, is often referred to as one indication of the expanding role of government. Recall that gross national product is the final market value of all goods and services produced in the economy in the course of one calendar year, at current market prices. The easy way to remember its components is to visualize the four big spenders: households, business, government and foreigners. The sum of personal consumption expenditures, government spending for goods and services, gross private domestic investment, and exports minus imports equals gross national product.

Government purchases of goods and services include those of state and local governments. Although total government purchases represent a large portion of the gross national product (23 percent in 1968), this is an inadequate indicator of the economic impact of government.

Several types of government spending are not included in this figure. All government transfer payments, such as social security benefits and welfare payments, are excluded. These

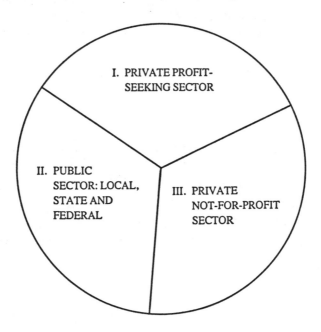

Figure 3-1   The three major sectors of the economy. This book deals with Sectors II and III.

Table 3-1 Government purchases of goods and services, by type, as a percent of gross national product. 1960-1977

Year	*Government Purchases of Goods and Services as a Percentage of Gross National Product.*		Federal		State and Local
			National Defense	*Non-defense*	
	Total	*Total*			
1960	19.8	10.6	8.8	1.8	9.2
1961	20.7	10.9	9.0	2.0	9.7
1962	20.9	11.3	9.1	2.3	9.6
1963	20.8	10.9	8.5	2.4	9.9
1964	20.4	10.3	7.7	2.5	10.2
1965	20.1	9.8	7.2	2.6	10.3
1966	21.1	10.5	8.0	2.5	10.6
1967	22.6	11.4	9.0	2.4	11.2
1968	22.9	11.3	8.9	2.4	11.6
1969	22.2	10.4	8.2	2.3	11.8
1970	22.3	9.7	7.5	2.3	12.5
1971	22.0	9.0	6.6	2.4	12.9
1972	22.0	8.7	6.3	2.4	12.9
1973	21.0	7.8	5.6	2.2	12.8
1974	21.4	7.9	5.4	2.4	13.6
1975	22.2	8.1	5.5	2.6	14.1
1976	21.2	7.6	5.1	2.5	13.5
1977	(provisional)				
	20.9	7.7	5.0	2.7	13.1

Source: *Economic Report of the President, 1978* (Washington, D.C., Government Printing Office, 1978) Table B-1.

payments are not made to compensate individuals for contributing supplies of factor services to the current output of goods and services. Interest payments made by government are also excluded on the grounds that the payments are not compensation to the owners of capital used in current production. Both the purchase of land by a government and the acquisition of financial assets, such as a veteran's mortgage, are arbitrarily excluded.

An additional type of public spending not included in government purchases of goods and services and, hence, missing from gross national product, is the payments made by public enterprises to cover current operating expenses. Government enterprises are defined as the agencies of government, both federal and state-local, whose operating costs are to a substantial extent covered by the sale of goods and services or the receipt of interest income. The Post Office and public power systems are typical examples. In essence, then, the current operations of government enterprises are treated in national income accounts as if they were private businesses. The value of the goods and services they produce is included in personal consumption

Table 3-2 Personal taxes and government transfer payments to persons as a percentage of personal income 1960-1976

Year	Federal, State and Local Personal Tax and Non-tax Receipts as a Percentage of Personal Income	Federal, State and Local Transfer Payments to Persons as a Percentage of Personal Income
1960	12.3	7.0
1961	12.3	7.6
1962	12.6	7.5
1963	12.6	7.6
1964	12.2	7.4
1965	11.6	7.1
1966	12.0	7.2
1967	12.6	7.8
1968	13.0	8.1
1969	14.8	8.4
1970	14.6	8.9
1971	13.2	10.2
1972	14.1	10.4
1973	13.6	10.5
1974	14.0	10.9
1975	13.7	12.6
1976	13.6	13.3

Source: *Economic Report of the President, 1978* (Washington, D.C., Government Printing Office, 1978) Table B-74 and B-75.

Table 3-3 Percentage of civilian labor force employed by government.

Year	Armed Forces	Federal	State and Local	Total
1960	.035	.031	.084	.150
1961	.035	.031	.086	.152
1962	.038	.031	.088	.157
1963	.037	.032	.092	.161
1964	.036	.031	.096	.163
1965	.035	.031	.100	.166
1966	.040	.032	.104	.176
1967	.043	.034	.107	.184
1968	.043	.033	.111	.186
1969	.042	.033	.112	.187
1970	.037	.032	.114	.183
1971	.032	.031	.117	.180
1972	.028	.030	.120	.178
1973	.026	.030	.122	.178
1974	.024	.029	.123	.176
1975	.023	.029	.126	.178
1976	.022	.028	.126	.176
1977	(provisional)			
	.021	.027	.125	.173

Source: *Economic Report of the President, 1978* (Washington D.C., Government Printing Office, 1978) Tables B-27 and B-34.

expenditures; most of the remainder represents an intermediate product purchased by other businesses.

Taxes as a percentage of gross national product are perhaps a better way of indicating the growth of the public sector. The percentage has grown from 27 percent of GNP in 1960 to 32 percent of GNP in 1977. This indicator may also be a bit misleading in measuring the size of the public sector. Table 3-2, contrary to indicating an expansion of government in the economy, demonstrates that government receipts collected from individuals did not increase significantly from 1960 to 1976. Furthermore, these receipts for the most part were transferred back to individuals and the transferred income is used for the most part to buy goods and services produced in the private sector.

Finally, employment data is an alternative way of looking at the relative importance of government (Table 3-3). Total government employment and its separate components—federal-military, federal-civilian and state-local—are shown as percentages of the total labor force. Twelve percent of the civilian labor force worked for government in nonmilitary positions in 1960 and fifteen percent in 1977. These figures for government employment include the employees of public enterprises, such as the Post Office and municipally-owned utilities.

Although it is impossible to come up with the perfect index for measuring the extent and growth of government activity in the economy, the data is sufficient to make the case that government is large.

The Size of the Private Not-For-Profit Sector

The private not-for-profit sector is likewise not a small part of the economy. Private schools of all types, churches, country clubs, unions, pension programs, Blue Cross and Blue Shield, research institutes and the YMCA are just a few of these enterprises. They are economic institutions because they provide a good or a service.

Private not-for-profit organizations accounted for 6.8 million jobs in 1973. This compares with the 14.7 million provided by government and 70 million in the profit-seeking sector. Hospitals and other medical and health services account for a large proportion of positions in the private not-for-profit sector.

What differentiates a private not-for-profit firm is its source of income. Mainly, they rely on a combination of sales, membership dues, contributions and grants from the private and public sectors. A hospital or a private university, for example, would depend for the most part on the sale of its products. Unions, however, rely almost exclusively on membership dues. The American Cancer Society receives virtually all of its funding from contributions and grants.

The fundamental accounting equation for a private profit-seeking firm (assets = liabilities + equity) is different from that of a private not-for-profit organization (assets = liabilities + funds). Most not-for-profit firms do not have equity or an ownership claim in the sense that a profit-seeking business would, except for some firms like credit unions, which are not-for-profit but where the members receive dividends. A fund is a separate accounting unit, the resources of which are used for specific activities.

The difference between revenues and expenses represents a change in fund balances. If positive, the sum is similar to the sum of dividends and retained earnings for a business firm; if negative, it is similar to a reduction in equity. Therefore, any surplus will be used to increase the growth of fund balances, but funds are also increased or decreased by the market value of their endowment investments.

Funds are often broken down into different categories. A church might have a building fund, an educational fund and a discretionary fund that the minister could use in an emergency to aid families in distress. Often there are restrictions on what can be done with certain assets in not-for-profit firms. For example, a family may donate an endowed chair to a University. The proceeds of this fund may only be used to pay the salary of one professor of outstanding merit. The actual investment may not be spent. The usual accounting treatment is to include the transaction as part of a special or restricted fund.

Private not-for-profit firms are often defined in terms of their tax status, the type of good they provide, and the sources of their financing. In some cases, these classifications demonstrate

differences between different types of private not-for-profit
firms better than they indicate the difference between this type
of firm and public or profit-seeking firms.

Private not-for-profit firms are tax exempt, for the most part,
and contributions to them are also tax exempt. The latter
exemption is probably more important than the former. Martin
Feldstein, an economist, estimated that contributions would
decrease by as much as forty percent if the deduction were
removed. However, some not-for-profit firms are really
profitable and would be affected by an income tax on profit, if
the profit could be defined. Currently, the federal tax laws
discourage not-for-profit firms from owning nonrelated profitable assets. They can lose their nonprofit status if too much
revenue comes from ancillary or commercial sources. Also,
they must pay taxes on such unrelated business.

It is probably not too cynical to suggest that some not-for-
profit firms are nonprofit precisely because of the tax laws.
However, justification of the legal nonprofit status is usually
made in terms of the type of good or service the firm is
providing. It should be mentioned, however, that not all not-for-
profit enterprises can be labeled as charitable or philanthropic
groups. Nor are all of these organizations characterized by the
production of what is called in economics a 'collective good.'

A collective good is one which cannot be divided among
members, excluding some and including others. For example,
we cannot allocate so many units of national defense to the
protecion of Barry Goldwater and take away some from Joan
Baez, who refused to pay taxes to be used for the Viet Nam War.
Often there is very little collectiveness associated with goods
produced in the not-for-profit sector. And even where there is a
collective element associated with the good, the benefit is
derived mostly by the club members and not society at large
which grants the legal nonprofit status.

The feature which most clearly differentiates not-for-profit firms from each other and from other firms is their source of income. Private not-for-profit firms in general receive 66% of their income from dues and assessments (Table 3-4); this is particularly the case with medical insurance plans and unions. Hospitals, which are most like profit-seeking concerns, receive most of their funding (94%) from sales. Some not-for-profit research institutions receive virtually all of their financing from the government and thus are little different from public organizations. The source of funding of a not-for-profit organization is perhaps the single most important factor in determining the behavior of the firm. The responsiveness of the firm will to a large degree be directly proportional to the sources of its financing.

The data, based on the Weisbrod and Long study, indicates the wide range in sources of financing for the private not-for-profit sector. In addition, the survey provides some clue to the size of the private, sometimes called voluntary, not-for-profit sector. Their survey indicates that the total revenue for all not-for-profit organizations was $530.9 billion in 1973.

This estimate should not be confused with gross national product. If the two figures were compatible, the private not-for-profit sector would equal 41 percent of GNP for 1973. But the estimate is not intended to represent that fraction of gross national product produced in this sector. Rather, it is merely the sum of the total revenue received by organizations in this sector. Thus the premium you pay to Blue Cross and Blue Shield which is later transferred to the hospital of your choice are both counted in this estimate. This, of course, involves double counting.

Unfortunately, at this time, data does not exist to estimate the value of goods produced in this sector (which could be compared directly to total GNP). Neither is it possible to break down the contributions, gifts, and grants going to these

Table 3-4 Voluntary Not-For-Profit Sector Revenue Sources, United States, 1973.

	(1) Religion		(2) Education		(3) Health		(4) Cultural		(5) Philanthropic Organizations (Sum of Columns 1-4)		(6) All Not-For-Profit Organizations	
(1) Sales and receipts	$2.8	(60%)	60.8	(65%)	31.1	(94%)	0.5	(45%)	95.2	(72%)	121.1	(23%)
(2) Dues and assessments	.2	(4%)	19.3	(21%)	0.2	(1%)	0.1	(9%)	19.8	(15%)	349.9	(66%)
(3) Contributions, gifts and grants	1.7	(36%)	13.2	(14%)	1.8	(5%)	0.5	(45%)	17.2	(13%)	59.9	(11%)
(4) Total revenue	4.7	(100%)	93.3	(100%)	33.1	(100%)	1.1	(100%)	132.2	(100%)	530.9	(100%)
(5) Percentage of total revenue for all (non-profit) organizations	0.8%		18%		6%		0.2%		25%		100%	
(6) Sample size	25		67		32		34		158		432	

Source: Burton A. Weisbrod and Stephen H. Long, "The Size of the Voluntary Nonprofit Sector: Concepts and Measures," Chapter 2 in Burton A. Weisbrod, *The Voluntary Nonprofit Sector* (D.C. Heath and Company, Lexington, Massachusetts, 1977) Table 2-3.

Note: Data, based on the calculations, are estimated national aggregates based on a random sample of 432 Form 990 tax returns, adjusted upwards for the approximately 650,000 nonprofit organizations.

Dollar amounts in billions. Figures in parentheses are percentages of total for each (column) subsector.

organizations between private and public sources. This information would be very helpful, because it would enable us to know the degree of overlap between the two not-for-profit sectors.

Why Such Growth in the Not-For-Profit Sector?

Maybe growth in this sector results from the feeling that profit is a dirty word. Maybe any organization that is not out to make a profit is considered to be better than one that is. Some people are turned off by the fact that Weight Watchers is a profit-seeking organization. It seems to these people that the organization is trying to take advantage of an individual's helplessness in dealing with obesity. The fact that the program is relatively effective and inexpensive is not important to those with an anti-profit-seeking bias.

In addition there is a prevailing assumption that whatever it is that a not-for-profit firm produces is somehow good for society. We tend to think that health care and education produced in a not-for-profit enterprise are somehow on a higher level than automobiles, pickles, and underwear produced in a profit-seeking firm.

If it really is the case that we tend to deal lightly with not-for-profit firms, it is necessary to demonstrate how this favoritism is expressed. The most apparent manifestation of this preferential treatment is in the Internal Revenue Code. There are great advantages to being legally a nonprofit organization, especially at a time when living, breathing, and moving are taxed.

Preferred tax status to non-stock corporations is specified in section 50l(c)(3) of the Internal Revenue Code. Eligibility includes numerous institutions which are organized and operated:

"...exclusively, for religious, charitable, scientific, testing for public safety, literary, or educational purposes or for the prevention of cruelty to children or animals, no part of the net earnings of which enures to the benefit of private shareholder or individual, no substantial part of the activities of which is carrying on propaganda or otherwise attempting to influence legislation and which does not participate in or intervene in any political campaign on behalf of any candidate for public office receives a preferred tax status."

In addition to special tax status in the form of an exemption from corporate income taxes, not-for-profit firms enjoy exemptions from various state, local, and federal taxes. They also benefit from tax deductibility of donor contributions and membership dues under certain circumstances. In addition, they qualify for special third class mailing privileges!

The growth of the public sector is to some extent described by Wagner's Law, named after a 19th century German economist. The law observes that governments inexorably grow larger and that the collective sector of an economy has an inherent tendency to increase in size and importance. Some explanations for this observed fact may be that as incomes increase, people's demand for all goods and services rise and perhaps the demand for public goods and services rises more than proportionally. In other words, the elasticity of demand for public goods with respect to income is positive.

Another argument often expressed is that population density necessitates increasingly interdependent life styles and public goods thus become more important. For example, it might be the case that law enforcement and social welfare programs are valued more by those living in a densely populated area. However, it might also be the case that it is not the density itself but the breakdown of family, community and private charity that creates a gap that government tries to fill.

Public choice theory attempts to explain how collective decisions are made and thus predicts from this approach the growth in the not-for-profit sector. In this context the theory suggests that when a group of individuals makes a collective decision, individuals agree to things they do not necessarily want in order to get what is personally significant to themselves. Sometimes, politicians go along (vote for a questionable proposal) to get along (to get votes for their own proposals). Thus the public not-for-profit sector expands.

4

ENDS VERSUS MEANS: A PUBLIC

GOODS APPROACH

The central problem in the administration of not-for-profit firms is the provision of public goods. Several political economists are developing a theory of collective action that is in marked contrast to the study of Public Administration in the United States. In the traditional Public Administration approach, idealistically, the public official knows what the people want or is explicitly told what the politician wants. The administrator then is expected to set aside all personal preferences to execute this mandate as effectively as possible. The public goods approach differs in several ways. It is characterized by its theory of behavior, its methodology, its definition of what is a public good, and the criterion it uses to measure the effectiveness of the organization.

The public goods approach to not-for-profit firms emphasizes first the existence of market failure in which the economically optimal amount of a particular good is over- or under-produced. In addition, the approach recognizes that not-for-profit firms may be created by groups of individuals to produce what is perceived by them to be socially desirable outcomes. The failures of the free market, or profit-seeking sector, are outlined in this chapter, and the concept of what constitutes a public good is introduced. However market failure is a necessary but not sufficient condition for production and provision by the not-for-profit sector. The not-for-profit sector, like its counterpart, is

itself subject to certain generic types of failure and these are
discussed in the second half of the chapter.

Market Failure and the Consequent Need for Public Goods and Services

The nature of public goods and services can best be understood by realizing how they are similar and different from
private goods. Private goods and services are freely purchased
in markets by individuals who are trying to get the best deal for
the amount paid from individuals who are trying to make the
most profit. If the exchange is consummated, we can assume
that both parties were satisfied. Public goods are generally
provided collectively, either in public or private not-for-profit
firms. Only indirectly through voting does one have any choice
over the type, amount and cost of the good or service.

Generally, when an auto mechanic wants strawberries, he
goes down to the local store and buys them. He could grow them
himself or, if he were very wealthy, hire a full-time gardener and
build a greenhouse in which to grow them. Evidently, it is easier
for him to earn money repairing cars and use the specialized
services of the supermarket. The advantages of doing this are
called the "gains from trade" or "specialization."

Similarly, the auto mechanic could hire a personal bodyguard
to protect himself on the streets at night or to guard his home,
and many individuals do so. However, there is some gain to
entering into a cooperative agreement with neighbors to have
this service produced collectively. All the houses on the street
could conceivably be protected by one guard. And certainly the
mechanic doesn't want to foot the whole bill to pay for this
guard, who would deter crooks coming to do damage to a
neighbor's house.

Thus, a community of individuals may decide to demand goods and services collectively rather than individually, precisely because the bilateral exchanges facilitated by market arrangements are insufficiently inclusive. In other words, agreement among all members of the community is deemed more efficient, because, once the street is protected, those who decided not to purchase the service would still enjoy the benefits.

The public goods approach to public administration recognizes the gain to be realized by entering into cooperative agreements. However, this approach emphasizes that the consumer cannot directly determine which type of public goods or services, or the precise amount to be provided, without complete unanimity, which is unlikely. But, the collective process for providing goods and services is justified when significant externalities exist. The issue of externalities is developed further in Chapter 8. Externalities exist when a third party receives benefits or bears costs arising from an economic transaction in which he or she is not a direct participant. Externalities are a clear instance of market failure.

Strawberries, for example, are fully paid for and fully enjoyed by the consumer and hence are best provided by free exchange in the market place. Safe streets, provided and paid for by a small group of neighbors, would yield benefits to non-members, and the cost proportional to benefits received by members could be extremely high. Hence the supply of safe streets has externalities associated with it and may best be provided publicly.

The second source of market failure is the existence of economies of large-scale production. Where increased output of a product in a firm is subject to declining marginal costs, a single producer may be the lowest cost method of production. The firm evolves into a profit-seeking monopolist which tends, according to economic theory, to limit output and raise price. A society may choose to ignore the wastes generated by natural monopolies, as the lesser of two evils, or, on the other hand, use government intervention to operate, to regulate, or to prohibit single-firm takeover.

The third source of market failure or friction may exist where the price, information and mobility characteristics are different from those necessary for efficient transactions. Finally, the outcome of a market process, particularly with respect to the distribution of income, may not be acceptable to some or even most of the individuals in the society. This is so even when the "winners" in the market process did not attain their positions by violating any laws or constitutional agreements.

The public goods approach to the not-for-profit sector stresses the ethical as well as economic legitimacy of the externality criteria, above other types of market failure, to determine if a good or service should be produced collectively. However, proponents of this approach are generally realistic enough to realize that the criteria of externalities will not always be applied correctly and often will be ignored. But if the not-for-profit sector, for political or historical reasons, gets involved in producing a private good with little externalities, the public goods approach gives primary consideration to the effectiveness of the agency in providing the good or service rather than to distributional or ethical considerations. Is the not-for-profit firm providing what it was created to provide?

Evaluating the Not-for-Profit Firm: A Rule of Thumb

Failure in the profit-seeking sector is due to the absence of certain market conditions needed for efficiency. Merely changing the firm to not-for-profit status will not ensure efficiency, and it may actually aggravate the problem. The failure of not-for-profit firms stems from an almost complete absence of any mechanism for reconciling the internal policy of the firm with successful provision of the public good or service.[1]

The public goods approach to administration in not-for-profit firms recognizes that the consumer's questions about performance are valid. Unfortunately, the mere presence of honest, well-educated individuals managing not-for-profit firms, doing what they perceive to be in the public interest, is no guarantee of effective performance. And, even if it were sufficient, there remains the problem of measuring the performance of a private or public not-for-profit firm.

Many argue that public goods are least able to be measured and, therefore, no attempt should be made. How do you measure amounts or quality of safety or learning? The argument has some merit but it is not consistent. In the private sector, how do you measure the value of a lawyer's advice or a physician's diagnosis? The answer, of course, is that one does not generally measure their output explicity, but rather takes his business elsewhere if unsatisfied with the service. Unfortunately, in the public not-for-profit sector one must either pay taxes or go to jail. Similarly, private not-for-profit firms package their provision of services with membership in the organization so that one must exit from the organization or bear up with a poorly produced service. The food, for example, at the country club may be poor, but because the setting is friendly and attractive and dues are prepaid one occasionally chooses to eat there, or changes clubs.

The public goods approach suggests that it may be possible to build alternatives into the provision of public goods. A voucher

[1]Charles Wolf, Jr., "A Theory of Nonmarket Failure: Framework for Implementation Analysis." *The Journal of Law and Economics* (April, 1979), pp. 107-139.

system, for example, would enable a taxpayer to purchase a publicly provided good or service or be reimbursed for that amount if he chooses to buy the same service privately. Private not-for-profit firms could fund some of their services separately from general membership dues.

However, this raises the question of duplication of services and overlapping jurisdictions. American public administration traditionally has concerned itself with reorganizing the structure of administrative relations in accordance with the principles of hierarchical organizations. We are taught to abhor the overlapping jurisdictions and fragmentation of authority inherent in the American political system. Yet institutional failure may accrue from the absence of such overlap rather than because of it. It is the absence of sustained competition that contributes to the difficulty of evaluating output quality.[2]

When the central problem in Public Administration is viewed as the provision of public goods and services, alternatives to a perfectly ordered bureaucratic structure may be needed. A beautiful structure may not provide the consumer with the best service. Particular types of public goods and services may best be provided jointly by the coordinated actions of a multiplicity of non-profit firms.

When a good Italian restaurant opens up in a town lined with fast food chains serving millions of morsels of indigestibility, few cry "needless duplication." Similarly, the duplication of bureaucracies may increase consumer satisfaction. Five state universities offering degrees in elementary education may be better than one. Duplication is not necessarily a vice. If the agency is accountable to the community of interest, if those who pay receive the benefits, and if it is operated in a manner acceptable to the community, the specialized or differentiated service offered by several agencies may outweigh any scale

[2]*Ibid.* p. 114

economies. All of this is to say that the "right" structure in public administration cannot be viewed apart from the process of choice.

In the federal government, the Department of State is first among equals in determining the direction of U.S. foreign policy with respect to a particular nation, but other Departments, such as Defense and Commerce, also have desk officers specializing in particular countries and have some input into policy formulation. This could be needless duplication of effort. Or, again, such scrutiny could be a check on the State Department which results in making foreign policy more consistent with the general aims of the American people.

However, competing agencies, each providing the same or a similar public good, present a problem that cannot be ignored. In the profit-seeking sector, a pizza shop with lousy pizza will not sell much and will either learn how to make good pizza or go out of business. There is no such automatic exit in the public sector. There might not even be a withering away or shrinking down of the worst of the agencies. Deaths of not-for-profit firms occur at a lower rate than profit-seeking business failures, but they do happen.

Note that no cabinet-level department has ever gone out of existence. However, on lower levels of the government bureaucracy there is much ferment and turnover. Similarly, colleges and universities tend to survive, but departments within them are periodically reviewed and sometimes axed. Not-for-profit firms sometimes survive by changing their function as in the well known case of the March of Dimes. Previously, the organization concerned itself with polio, now controllable, and currently deals with birth defects. In the not-for-profit sector, the equivalent of bankruptcy does not exist!

In conclusion, the not-for-profit firm may be the correct antidote for market failure, but not-for-profit firms are protected from competition and elimination of the least effective firms is not guaranteed. Furthermore, they deal in a product, the output and quality of which is virtually impossible to measure. But accountable they must be: Are they producing what they were intended to provide?

PART II

THE POWER

5

HOW ADMINISTRATORS BEHAVE

(ARE THEY HUMAN?)

A group of individuals must decide what it wants done, set up a firm to provide the good or service, and then look around for an administrator. Now if there were a surplus of brilliant, well-trained, selfless and scrupulously honest individuals (like you and me), willing to do this work at a "reasonable" wage, there would be no problem in finding an administrator. Alas, there just are not enough of us to go around. And, in a more humble moment, even the authors would admit that there have been times and situations (very few you understand) when they have not operated quite so admirably.

So most not-for-profit firms are staffed with persons who at times are capable of greatness, but who in general can be expected to operate in a very ordinary manner. Thus, to determine beforehand what the group of individuals may expect to receive for its dollar, it might be well to develop a theory of behavior that is realistic.

A Theory of Human Behavior

There is no reason to believe that officials of not-for-profit firms act differently than any other group of individuals. And, although it is impossible to say how one individual responds, in general, people operate in their own self-interest.

Man does not change his nature because he is submerged in a not-for-profit firm. He remains an individual, with individual motives, impulses, and longings. Much of administrative theory is based on the contrary view that man becomes a machine when he is placed within a hierarchy. This machine is expected to faithfully carry out the orders of superiors, and these superiors are expected to act in the interest of society in reaching policy decisions.

As long as the theory of the not-for-profit firm refuses to recognize the cruder instincts in man of acquisitiveness and self-preservation, it will fail to create not-for-profit firms that direct these characteristics toward the goal of the firm. Consequently, it will be forced to rely on the noble but scarce virtues of benevolence and self-sacrifice. And if self-interest explains best how all men act, the traditional study of Public Administration will fail to formulate meaningful propositions.

The student might, at this point, suggest that it is better to end up disillusioned than to initially develop a system based on the assumption that administrators are greedy. It must be rememberd that this assumption does not say that all public officials are lying crooks! Rather, the initial statement about human behavior in most economic theory is that individuals make decisions based on their own self-interest. Hence, we should proceed with the study of administration on the assumption that the fundamental laws of human behavior are the same for individuals operating in the not-for-profit as well as in the profit-seeking sector.

As children we were told that police officers were our friends; they helped us cross streets and bought us ice cream when we were lost. In the scheme of things, they were just a notch lower than Santa Claus and on the same level as grandparents. With the increased sophistication and experience (such as receiving tickets for speeding, obsolete inspection tags, etc.), we came to suspect that only power happy, gun loving individuals would do such a job. Hence, we agree that most officers are "on the take." Each of these images is as incorrect as the other, which is not to say that police forces do not contain both types of individuals.

But the representative police officer, like the representative physician or hair stylist, works at law enforcement because he or she sees it as the best and easiest way for them to make a good living. Note, it certainly may not be the easiest way for us to make a living, but then most of us have not chosen to be police officers.

Managers in profit-seeking firms are constrained by market forces from co-opting the firm for their own purposes. If internal decisions are not consistent with the interest of the stockholders and customers, profits and the market value of its stock will decline. The feedback is not always perfect in a profit-seeking firm, but nothing similar exists for the not-for-profit firm. Therefore, administrators, employees, or perhaps a subset of consumers may attempt and succeed in taking over a firm that was created to serve a public purpose. The issue is not whether the firm is producing something "good" but rather whether it is producing what was "intended."

Methodology

No doubt everyone has read stories about the anxiety that Einstein felt when he realized the ends, namely, atomic destruction, to which his scientific theory was applied. A similar type of dismay must confront those who systematically study efficiency in the not-for-profit sector. Nazi Germany and Jonestown, Guyana were, at least in the short-run, reasonably effective not-for-profit firms carrying out the will of their dictators. When such firms are effective, due to unlimited resources and the coercive force of authority, the misery inflicted on humankind may be catastrophic. Mindful of this danger, we nevertheless proceed with a method of analyzing how to anticipate and adjust for ineffectiveness in the not-for-profit firm.

Based on the behavior of the average or representative unit or individual, a theory of a descriptive or explanatory nature about not-for-profit firms may be formulated. For example, if we first assume that administrators in these firms act as others do in trying to earn income and advancing their careers and, secondly, assume that the clients of not-for-profit firms try to maximize their satisfaction subject to the individual price paid for these services, predictions may be made concerning how most individuals will respond in given institutional situations. The validity of the theory will depend on how well it assists us in our understanding of the operations of bureaucratic systems. Idealistically, the anticipation of failure can be a valuable tool for avoiding outright mistakes.

Consider the case of the small town, the citizens of which have decided through some voting process to develop a recreational program. Large amounts of money are allocated to the program, the best trained recreational personnel are hired, and it is clearly defined organizationally to whom the agency reports. However, unless further checks and incentives are built into the program, we could hypothesize that the recreational program will operate from nine to five, Monday through Friday, and will submit a larger budget for the following year ''in order to better meet the needs of the community.'' Some individuals in the community, namely those that scream the loudest, may actually be able to get the organization to operate in their behalf. For example, when tennis is in vogue, much of the budget will be allocated to that sport, which may result in an overbuilding of tennis courts.

A realistic theory of the not-for-profit firm, if properly employed, may serve as a guide to the development of agencies that actually achieve the objective of providing a public good. As such, this theory of administration falls within the discipline of managerial science in the not-for-profit sector. The essential problem in administration then is to anticipate consequences when self-interested individuals choose maximizing strategies within particular not-for-profit organizations.

At this point, we would like to issue a word of caution on current techniques used to determine agency effectiveness. First of all, some of the literature in this area assumes that because contented workers are more productive we can survey the workers in a not-for-profit firm and assume that if they are reasonably content then the agency is effective! It may be the case that malcontents do not produce but this does not imply that contented individuals perform in the intended manner.

A second attempt to oversimplify the problem of effectiveness in not-for-profit firms, is the great reliance on client surveys. Surveys are great release valves and are to some extent informative. However, they are a poor substitute for the choice that one has in the profit-seeking sector. Surveys of the satisfaction rates of users of a not-for-profit agency are usually biased upwards. This is particularly the case when the product is being subsidized out of general tax revenue. It is difficult to be dissatisfied with getting something at less than full cost. An additional problem with surveys is that too often the respondent has little to gain personally from a careful and honest evaluation of the not-for-profit firm or employee.

Finally, mistaken attempts, discussed at length in Chapter 18, are oftentimes made to measure quantitatively the productivity of employees in not-for-profit firms. If, however, administrators come up with an inappropriate measure, the whole plan backfires as people pump out what is measured, even if this is detrimental to the overall object of the firm.

In conclusion, students of administration deal with the same individuals in profit-seeking and not-for-profit firms. Initially, one should proceed on the assumption that the fundamental law of behavior, namely self-interest, is the same under both sets of institutions. Working with these behavioral assumptions, hypotheses can be developed that will assist us in understanding, and thus avoiding failure, in the operations of not-for-profit firms.

6

THE MISSING GAP IN MANAGERIAL

DISCRETION

It is undoubtedly reasonable to assume that profit-seeking firms try to increase their profits. Furthermore, there is no need to apologize for this objective. In fact, economic theoreticians suggest benefits for all of society, in general, when managers seek to maximize profits. On the other hand, when a firm attempts to exercise "social responsibility" (as opposed to maximizing profits), who decides if this means higher prices and less pollution, neighborhood clean-up projects, or the employment of less qualified but minority workers? Indeed, how can one measure the achievement of social responsibility? Not all would agree, but perhaps in the profit-seeking sector "minding the store" *should* unabashedly be identified with maximizing profits.

Does it also follow that the not-for-profit firm should be in the business of losing money (perhaps maximizing losses)? This, unfortunately, is not a bad description of what is done in practice. However, the opinion expressed in this book is that the not-for-profit firm *should* be in the business of producing a good or service, preferably not ones produced in the profit sector, and *should* be doing this as effectively as possible.

The case will be made that the best explanation of what profit-seeking firms do is attempt to increase profits but that a different explanation is needed to describe what not-for-profit firms attempt. A model, generally known as the behavioral theory of the firm or the theory of managerial discretion, is presented as a good explanation of what a not-for-profit firm does.

The Simple Assumption of Profit Maximization

Profit maximizing theory is concerned neither with the largest average nor the largest marginal profit. Nothing less than maximum total profit is accepted as a goal. A firm profit maximizes when its marginal cost and its marginal revenue are equal. The pizza producer keeps making pizza and selling it for, let us say $4, as long as each additional pizza costs less than $4 to make. This profit-seeking firm is choosing input and output combinations from those in its feasible set in order to equate marginal revenue and marginal cost.

This theoretical firm, however, has few of the characteristics which management analysts find in the real world of pizza makers. In theory, there is no mention of the organization of the firm, there are no control problems in the enterprise, it has no aspiring managers, and it has no standard operating procedures.

On what basis is it reasonable to assert that a firm is merely profit maximizing rather than engaging in sales or revenue maximization? Theoretical justification for such an assumption often relies on *Occam's Razor*. This sharp-edged rule of Occam, a fourteenth century scholastic, states that in any system the number of unconnected propositions and those for which there are no proof should be at a minimum. Thus, in deciding between two explanations for the same phenomenon, the one which requires fewer simplifying assumptions should be chosen. In other words, most people who are fat eat too much. Other more complicated explanations of obesity usually add little to the understanding of the phenomenon.

When the external environment in which a firm operates is extremely competitive, it is generally redundant to enrich the theory. Enriching the theory refers to adding additional explanations to the argument of what a firm tries to do. For example, it could be hypothesized that a firm attempts to increase its share of the market, maximize sales, mold public support for the firm, upgrade the local community, and promote social justice. Economists generally agree that the extension and enrichment of the objective of the firm is important and useful, but under the pressure of competition, these alternate explanations of what a firm does reveals very little.

It would certainly be foolish to include in an objective function to be maximized all the attractive sounding goals one could think of as possibly being relevant to a firm. Maybe the optimum managerial decisions would be the same no matter which of a number of objectives the firm would choose to pursue. Thus, it is certainly legitimate in economic analysis to pare down the objectives of a firm if the multiplicity of objectives all lead to the same optimum decision. This, in fact, seems to be one of the reasons for sticking so closely to profit maximization as a single theoretical goal in classical microeconomics.

Outlining too many determinates or causes may not be very helpful as the following example illustrates. A commission was set up to study why the performance of seniors in high school on college entrance tests declined each year from 1967 onwards. The results of the study were anxiously awaited by educators and the public, in general, and the press scrutinized the report. The report suggested that the reasons for the decline, among other things, were the Vietnamese War; the draft; the fact that more students were taking the tests and thus dragging down the average; the disruption of family life; television; and a decreasing emphasis on basic skills. Undeniably, each of these things are in some way related to the issue. The report was unsatisfactory, however, in the sense that it did not go any further in isolating causes and explaining the phenomenon than would a group of individuals at a dinner party.

This book, however, deals with not-for-profit firms. These firms provide a particular circumstance where goals may be added to the objective function not just for realism, but to explain a behavioral situation. In this case, the profit maximizing objective either does not exist or is not a reasonable proxy for explaining the decisions of such firms. Therefore, the purpose in adding other arguments to the objective function is not that of added realism, but rather a replacement of a profit maximizing goal which is not present in not-for-profit firms.

Expanding the Objective Function

Although not-for-profit firms do not maximize profits, what they actually do has generally been ignored. It is in this realm, however, that expansion and enrichment of the goals of the firm is certainly valid. The notion that managers make decisions which lead to goals other than the maximization of profit *or the public interest* is central to understanding the not-for-profit firm. The vaguely stated organizational objective of most not-for-profit firms leaves the managers little more than a slogan in the way of a concrete objective.

A subgoal is a secondary goal which should not be pursued if it interferes with a primary goal of the organization. However, administrators with vaguely stated objectives may begin to pursue subgoals, just as lower level managers in large enterprises are led to pursue goals not necessarily in consonance with profit maximization. Thus while large organizations might experience subgoal pursuit among their managers due to malcoordination, the not-for-profit firm will certainly encounter it whenever a clearly operative enterprise-wide objective is lacking. For example, the director of a recreational program in a small town may be given a budget and told to aid the town in the physical fitness of its citizens. The administrator of the recreational program may implicitly assume that the goals of the program are identical to whatever he or she believes physical fitness to be.

While profit maximizing economic theory concentrates on the ends of the enterprise, managerial discretion theory concentrates on the personal goals of the managers of the organization. The purpose of the following model is to make explicit the motivations of managers and expand the concept of enterprise objectives. This will provide the more general basis needed for examination of the not-for-profit firm.

Organizations cannot think or act, but people within organizations can act subject to certain constraints placed on them by the characteristics of the organization in which they operate. This model assumes that administrators strive to maximize their own well-being. However, the administrator in a particular not-for-profit firm must produce at some minimum level of performance. Otherwise, they will be fired. The performance level cannot be defined precisely; it is implicit rather than explicit. In other words, it is that minimum level of service that the sponsoring organization will tolerate without revolting. This sponsor revolt could take the form of a reduced budget, closer scrutiny of day-to-day operations in the firm, slashing of perks enjoyed by the staff, loss of staff, or even a friendly suggestion that the administrator resign.

The model operates in the following way. Managers or administrators of not-for-profit firms like to increase the size of their staff to make their lives easier and justify their salaries. They also like managerial emoluments such as meals, with or without three martinis, convention jaunts, use of the firm's plane, and long-distance telephone services. These managerial perks are particularly important in not-for-profit firms, where salaries at the top are less than in the private proft-seeking sector. Moreover, administrators would like to expend at their discretion any budgetary surplus over that needed to provide the minimum level of service.

Administrators in not-for-profit firms try to maximize, among other things, the gap between the funds that they actually need to perform the minimum level of service expected and the total size of the budget. This gap should not be viewed as quasi-profit. In the first place, the administrators have no ownership rights to this residual. True enough, it could revert back to the sponsoring organization and the budget reduced the following year; however, it would be difficult to come up with examples of where and when this has ever happened.

Secondly, if this gap is negative it is often used to justify a higher budget for the same level of service the following year. In a negative profit case, the profit-seeking firm would either have to improve its service or go out of business.

It should also be emphasized at this point that administrators of not-for-profit firms do not make it a point to publish an annual report indicating the amount of their surplus budget! In fact, they go to great lengths to disguise it. This is done by increasing staff, emoluments and other things to make the life of not-for-profit administrators more comfortable.

It is important to note also that if the sponsoring organization and their constituency has high expectations about the level of service and a fair idea of how much it costs to provide those services, administrators will have to do with adequate staffs, productive emoluments and few purely discretionary funds. In other words, they will operate efficiently in the full economic sense of the word.

In conclusion, there are three key concepts in the managerial discretion model which justify its application to not-for-profit firms in general. First of all, the model recognizes the possibility that administrators exert discretion over the level of goods and services produced. Secondly, the model assumes that the level of services must not fall below some specified minimum, at the risk of intervention from the sponsor into the activities of the administration. And, finally, the model demonstrates that administrators spend as they see fit any excess funds on additional staff or managerial emoluments. It is assumed, furthermore, that administrators prefer bigger budgets, more staff and larger managerial emoluments.

7

WHO'S REALLY IN CHARGE?

Telling people what to do and seeing that they do it is identified as the directing phase of management. The manager has plans that he wants carried out, and must, therefore, divide the work and hire people who are capable of doing it. In addition, he must compel or induce people to use their talents.

To carry out this function, it is essential that the administrator have the power to reward and punish. Administrators may give or withhold raises and promotions, dismiss the recalcitrant, or lay off an employee temporarily without pay. Seldom, however, do administrators in the not-for-profit sector have these powers. The most the administrator can do is make recommendations that carry weight in determining promotion, salary and tenure. Perhaps the administrator can hassle or make life a little more difficult for a subordinate. Often, however, the subordinate has more leisure and tools to make life difficult for the head.

Constrained by limited power, the central problem facing administrators in the not-for-profit sector is that of increasing the number of decisions taken by subordinates that do, in fact, carry out the general policy of the whole organization. With the existence of managerial discretion and the pursuit of subgoals, the administrator's problem is to get subordinates to do what the organization requires. As a first step, the head must communicate his desires and see that these are carried out.

Hup, Two, Three, Four

John Fitzgerald Kennedy, in an interview two years after he had assumed the Presidency, noted that when he was in the Congress he felt frustrated because all power seemed to reside in the White House. Now, from the White House, it seemed to him that all power originated from the Hill. Similarly, the administrators of not-for-profit firms, particularly large ones, often feel that the higher up they go in an organization the less power they have. An interesting question is the extent to which a particular not-for-profit firm reflects the basic philosophy and approach of the chief administrator. Is it the case that Harvard is Harvard because Derek Bok is its president? Or is Princeton Princeton because William Bowen is its president?

Woodrow Wilson, a student of administration, assumed that in any organization there is a center of power. Once this center is identified, the structure of authority can be unravelled and the symmetry of social life in that political community understood. In other words, if you were to feel you were getting the bureaucratic run around, you could step back and figure out who really calls the shots in the agency and proceed from there to deal more effectively with the bureau.

If, indeed, a center of power exists, public administration can limit its analysis to the reorganization of not-for-profit firms according to the principles of hierarchical organization. Unity of command, span of control, departmentalization by major functions, and direction by single heads of authority in subordinate units, have universal applicability. It has been thought that the application of these concepts would result in perfecting administrative arrangements.

Max Weber, a German sociologist and political economist, born in 1864, conceived of a hierarchically ordered system of administration which he indentified as "bureaucracy." In this system, the bureaucrat generally follows faithfully all orders coming from above, even if such orders are against his personal opinions and beliefs. Insofar as general policy making is concerned, the bureaucrat is a mere tool; he should put aside his own preferences and execute in a highly "neutral" manner his superior's will. Weber's theory of bureaucracy is fully consistent with the traditional theory of administration in both form and method.

The image of this type of bureaucracy, according to Gordon Tullock, a political economist, can be likened to that of a troop of bureaucrats on a drill field marching in perfect regimentation. The chief administrator shouts "Left!" and all turn. He later shouts "Right!" and they all turn on command. Attempts to try to duplicate this situation in all not-for-profit firms are certainly unrealistic and may even be inefficient in terms of the effective provision of the good or service.

In 1946, Herbert Simon contended that the chain of command as expressed in the traditional theory of Administration was logically inconsistent with technical competencies. In other words, the chief administrator of a hospital with his or her degree in administration had better not direct the staff physicians in brain surgery.

Simon developed efficiency criteria such that if the benefits from relaxing the chain of command exceeded the costs, then efficiency would be served by relaxing the chain of command. The problem, however, is to identify the efficiency criteria. Whose interests are violated when the chain of command is broken? Speculate on a situation in which a local welfare worker spends an afternoon, at his or her discretion, helping a client. Together, the client and the social worker work through the red tape of a particular problem, not included in the social worker's job description. The particular client may benefit but the rest of the worker's case load might bear the cost. There is no doubt that the chain of command has been violated.

Similar situations exist in the profit-seeking sector but it is generally easier for lower level employees to resolve them. For example, a waiter or a waitress may give extra service to a family by cutting the meat and in general helping out with the children. Since the family is a paying customer, there are likely future benefits (a bigger tip) if the family decides to frequent the restaurant. At the same time, however, the waiter or waitress will be very careful not to offend other paying customers. The extra service will only be provided to the family if time permits. The trade off in providing service to two different customers is rather explicit to a subordinate when the customers are paying for the service.

Procedures and Layering

One apparent mechanism to get subordinates to carry through on their assignments, in the manner expected, is to provide the employee with procedures detailing how to handle every situation he or she could possibly confront. In addition, one could develop a network whereby the explicit goals and opinions of those at the top filter down to the executers of the policy.

But, have you ever played "telephone?" This is a game in which one person is given a message that he transmits to another person who in turn passes it on to another. At parties, the game is usually not played straight and there is a conscious attempt to scramble the message to get laughs. But even when the game is played straight, information is seldom passed without some interpretation, correct or incorrect. Our purpose is not to discount procedure manuals, but to emphasize the difficulty of interpretation.

The problem of filtering information up through administrative layers is equally difficult. Many administrators feel at times as if a glass wall had been built around them. They are consciously aware of their ignorance concerning details of the operation they are supposedly controlling. Furthermore, in large organizations it is virtually impossible to pass all information up or down the line.

For example, each lowly desk officer in the Department of Commerce in Washington is permitted to write a one or two paragraph statement of what he or she considers to be significant developments in his or her area of responsibility during the previous week. The section head decides which of these memos to pass on to the division head, who decides which will be passed on to the director of the organization. The director will select those that go to the head of the Bureau. The bureau head will decide which memos go on to the Secretary of Commerce, who will determine which go on to the White House for the enlightenment of the President. It should also be mentioned that new memos will be added at each level in addition to those deleted. Solutions on how to handle problems come down a similar route.

The information problem in any large not-for-profit firm is enormous. The problem of direction and supervision is almost beyond comprehension. Is there a solution? Yes, if the head realizes that his or her principal problem in achieving organizational efficiency is to arrange *the structure* so that subordinates reach a decision which the head would have reached given the particular situation. The administrator should not attempt to centralize decision making directly, but rather should influence his subordinates to make decisions that fit into the general design of the organization as the head administrator sees it.

Many bureaucracies exist which are out of control and which, consequently, are not really performing the function for which they were organized. In general, the larger the organization is, the smaller is the percentage of actions which reflect the administrators of the organization. What then do people do in large bureaucracies? They are doing first what they have to do to survive, and secondly, what they want to do.

Can such a system ever work to provide a community with the service it wished for in creating the agency? It can under two conditions. If the firm is somehow directly accountable to the relevant community of interest, there is a high probability that the agency will be responsive. In other words, *the not-for-profit firm needs close monitoring but it must be done by those who have the most to lose by poor performance of the firm.* But it is not often clear who this group is! It may be the users, or it may be the sponsors if the goal is a transfer of some kind. A police force is best monitored by the community as a whole and, in some instances, a school by it users. But certainly an adoption or welfare agency should, in terms of economic efficiency, be accountable to some group other than the recipient.

Secondly, *those not-for-profit firms will be effective which are financed in such a way that they are rewarded for how well they provide the intended good or service.* A firm which is granted a budget regardless of its degree of effectiveness will not operate effectively.

Increasing the probability of getting subordinates to solve problems in a way similar to the head has generally been solved by assigning positions to those persons with the same values or interests as the chief administrator. In many small owner-managed firms the most competent person is hired to do most jobs, except handle the cash register. That job is reserved for a relative. Companies recruit graduates of certain schools, personality types, and those who dress in a certain way. These proxies are used to insure the hiring of persons who will most likely do the job the way management wants it done. Affirmative action, on the other hand, generally supports hiring idealistically on the basis of objective criteria or, viewed less idealistically, on the basis of quota.

Cronyism, the old boy network, and nepotism are in one sense despicable and contrary to efficiency in any firm. Institutionalizing advantages for one or another particular subgroup of a society, either the haves or have nots, limits the pool from which qualified applicants can be drawn. But we tolerate it in particular instances. When the President appoints his brother Attorney General or when the mayor appoints his brother fire chief we tend to turn our heads. Along with our fear of the spoils system is the conflicting feeling that the coach should be able to choose his own team, because he will win more games if he is allowed to do so! And, after a few losing seasons, we can always fire him. This, of course, is the key to the dilemma. *If* the head as well as the staff can be made accountable *and* removed with little cost, the efficient alternative is to permit the chief administrator to hire his staff, with minimum constraints.

Administrative Hypocrisy

Sometimes the agency is doing exactly what the chief administrator wants. It is just from the point of view of the outsider that the bureau seems to be chaotic or off target.

It might be in the best interests of the head, particularly if he is politically appointed, to make it *appear* that a particular policy came from a lower level when it did not. In addition, it is not infrequent that the ''official policy'' of an organization differs sharply from its real policy.

At graduation ceremonies, the president of a university may express his commitment to the ''highest standards of academic excellence.'' But it may be wise to caution conscientious faculty members not to interpret that comment too literally!

PART III

THE PRODUCT

8

WHAT A PROFIT-SEEKING FIRM CANNOT

PROVIDE

There are few things in life which are certain; one of them is that virtually no one is pleased with the amount of goods provided collectively in not-for-profit firms, either private or governmental. Some think that the government provides too few services and they long for more public parks, symphonies, medical care and transportation. Other individuals think that the government has no business providing any of these things, and they would like to see the government wither away. Finally, some think that the amount of public goods is just right; however, the composition of the package of public goods provided is not appropriate. What is really needed, in their opinion, is less bombs and more downtown fountains. Others think the complete opposite.

Economic theory frankly admits that some goods cannot be provided by profit-seeking firms and, in addition, presents us with mathematical demonstrations of the impossibility of pleasing everyone.[1] Theory also provides us with a framework for carefully analyzing whether a good will be over- or under-produced by groups of firms operating in their own best interest. The reason for the existence of most not-for-profit firms is to provide those goods and services that the private profit-seeking

[1]J. M. Buchanan and G. Tullock, *The Calculus of Consent.*
Ann Arbor: Univ. of Michigan Press, 1962 and
J.M. Buchanan, *The Limits of Liberty*. Chicago: Univ. of Chicago Press, 1975.

sector cannot. An extension of the output theory of firms to not-for-profit firms is presented in Chapter 12.

Any given society will choose to produce some public goods and not others. In many instances, a society will decide through collective action or the will of a dictator to produce not only public goods but private goods as well. This chapter will first discuss public goods, in general, and secondly the process of choice in producing goods collectively.

Public Goods, Externalities and Property Rights

Public goods, in their pure form, are sometimes called collective or social goods. Paved roads and police protection are examples of public goods. Generally, these goods are not provided in the market by profit-seeking firms. People may desire these goods as strongly as private goods, but something inherent in the nature of public goods does not permit them to be provided in the market. There is a fundamental difference between private and public goods. A person cannot use a private good unless and until he or she pays for it. The good is not available to that individual until payment is made or some payment plan is agreed upon. Once a public good is provided, however, no one can be excluded from its benefits. Once a lighthouse is built, for example, all ships in the area are warned of danger from rocks or sandbars. There is no way that the light can be available only to those ships that paid for the lighthouse.

If a public good is to be provided, it must be provided through collective action or by someone generous enough to provide the good. This generous individual, of course, would personally receive a fraction of the benefits for which he or she paid. Needless to say, such generosity is rare.

In addition to pure public goods are goods that could be called mixed or quasi-public goods. These are goods that involve external costs or external benefits. *Externalities* are the positive or negative effects which transactions have on people who did not choose to participate in the exchange; they are third-party effects. A negative externality is called a *social cost*. Pollution is an example of a social cost.

The profit-seeking firm which produces a good or service, the production of which results in pollution, does not heed the costs inflicted on the public. The explicit or accounting costs upon which the firm bases its decision to produce more of the product do not reflect total costs, which is the sum of private and social costs. The consumers of these products therefore do not have to pay for the social costs, and, consequently, a decision to consume more of these goods is independent of the costs that society as a whole will bear. In the absence of emission controls, neither the producer of an automobile nor the consumer would voluntarily control the pollution that resulted from its production and use.

A positive externality is called a *social benefit*. When some individuals voluntarily follow a code of honesty, keep their homes well attended, and vaccinate themselves against infection, all of us receive something for which we did not pay. Most individuals unconsciously reduce their consumption of goods with large social benefits. On the other hand, if individuals were to be compensated in some way for that portion of the good which benefits the public, more goods with social benefits would be produced and consumed.

Figure 8-1 is an attempt to demonstrate the problem of the "correct" amount of public goods from a macroeconomic point of view. The curved line AA represents the production and consumption alternatives of a society at this point in time, given existing technology, resources and full employment. Any point

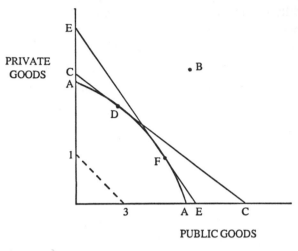

PUBLIC GOODS

FIGURE 8-1

within the axes and under or on the curve represents production alternatives; any point outside the curve such as point B is a production impossibility given the assumptions. The line CC is the ratio of the prices of public versus private goods. Note that public goods are approximately 3 times as expensive as private goods in this particular example. (The dotted line near the origin, which has the same slope as line CC, indicates a three-to-one price relationship.) All other things being equal, a society will substitute lower priced goods for higher priced ones, and point D represents the amount of private versus public goods that will be produced and consumed.

Recall, however, that, if there are significant negative externalities (social costs) associated with the production of private goods, market prices will not represent these costs. Consequently, in this example, there is an over-allocation of society's scarce resources towards private goods. If, on the other hand, those private goods that create social costs are taxed and those public goods that create social benefits are subsidized, then a new price line EE would be the relevant one for the consuming public, and point F would represent the "correct" allocation between public and private goods.

By what authority, however, should any government, community or club go about taxing what is "wrong" and subsidizing what is "right?" There is no easy answer to this question, but there is one that is worth considering. The assignment of property rights, or a clearer statement of the property rights, can shed some light on these problems. *Property rights* refers to the legal definition and protection given to the acquisition, holding, and transfer of ownership. When property rights are unassigned or are held communally, anyone can use the property without paying for its use so long as no one else is already using it.

There are resources, such as air and water, the boundaries of which are difficult to identify and divide. No one has property rights to the air surrounding them. Air is a resource where the property rights are indefinite or nonexistent. Unfortunately, when no one owns a particular resource, people do not have very much incentive to conserve on its use. And even if one person decides not to pollute the air, approximately the same amount of air pollution will remain. There are many other polluters.

The halls of condominium apartment houses, in the absence of strictly enforced laws, will tend to fill up with bikes, baby carriages and soda bottles (i.e. pollution). The inside of a particular apartment may be messy or neat, but even if it is messy we cannot say that it is polluted. Condominium apartment units are the property of individuals, and they may choose to keep their apartments as neat as they wish given their preferences or tolerances for messiness. When property rights hold, individuals have legal recourse to any damages sustained through the misuse of their property. When property rights are well-defined, the use of property—that is, the use of resources—will generally involve contracting between the owners of those resources. If you own an apartment house, you might contract with another person who wants to live in it. The contract would be written in the form of a rental agreement and in it would, hopefully, be clearly specified the rights and responsibilities of the owner and the renter.

A discussion of property rights is germane to the theory of the not-for-profit firm for two reasons. First, when significant externalities exist, an attempt may be made to rectify over- or under-allocation by the market place through the use of not-for-profit firms. For example, if it is believed that many will benefit from the learning of others, society may wish to subsidize educational institutions. Secondly, an understanding of property rights will shed much light on how individuals operate in any organization.

The absence of clearly specified property rights is the major cause of ineffectiveness in not-for-profit firms. In spite of anti-ownership sentiment, ownership is often a guiding force toward effectiveness. Ownership can provide an effective monitoring function. Not-for-profit educational institutions, credit unions and cooperatives of all types are sometimes very effective and efficient precisely because they are effectively monitored by an organization that has something at stake in the survival of the institution. Members of the organization are reluctant to permit the assets, tangible or intangible, and the reputation of the institution to be squandered in the interest of the users, workers or outside pressure groups.

Public Choice

Collective provision is one solution to the inability of the market to provide pure public goods and to the tendency to under-produce quasi-public goods. In other words, a group of individuals may agree, through some decision process, to tax themselves and use the proceeds to buy or produce public goods.

The membership of a labor union, for example, may decide to provide themselves with collective bargaining with the dues collected in general from the membership. Two points need to be emphasized. First, the decision to provide a good collectively does not imply that the group must produce the good. Rather it may purchase the good from a profit-seeking firm and merely provide it to its members. The union, for example, may hire experts in collective bargaining from another agency. Second, oftentimes the decision process in not-for-profit organizations does not limit itself to the provision of those goods unavailable or underproduced in the market. A union may purchase and operate a vacation resort for its members. Unless there is complete and total unanimity on the good to be provided collectively, the group is engaging to some extent in the involuntary transfer of resources among its members.

Decisions in unions and other not-for-profit organizations are often based on a simple majortiy; that is, an issue is approved if more than half vote affirmatively. Taking a vote on even the most complex matter is relatively easy. However, in many cases where this voting rule is applied, approximately 49 percent of the group is overruled. The extent to which the minority is harmed by a vote that went ''the other way'' varies. It may range from a little in things that are not significant, like the color on the union seal, or to great loss, if the union votes to go on strike for a few months.

One obvious way to minimize the number of losers is to increase the percentage needed to pass on important decisions. Or the organization could agree simply not to move in any direction until total unanimity is reached. The status quo, however, is not attractive when, in the case of public goods, the market is incapable of provision.

Futher complicating the decision to provide goods collectively is a phenomenon know as the *voting paradox*. A simple example might concern a student body deciding by vote how to allocate student health funds. A small student body composed of only three students (Jane, Tom and Alex) decides to employ the services of a medical specialist on campus one morning per week. Let us suppose that the students have the following personal preferences:

Jane prefers the gynecologist to a dermatologist and prefers a dermatologist to an orthopedist.

Tom prefers a dermatologist to an orthopedist and prefers an orthopedist to a gynecologist.

Alex prefers an orthopedist to a gynecologist and prefers a gynecologist to a dermatologist.

At the beginning of the Fall semester, students are polled on whether they wish to employ a gynecologist or a dermatologist. Referencing the preferences listed above—Jane votes for the gynecologist, Tom for the dermatologist, and Alex for the gynecologist. The gynecologist is selected by majority vote.

Second semester finds the student body with additional funds and they poll the students to determine whether they would now like a dermatologist or an orthopedist. Again referencing the preferences above—Jane votes for the dermatologist, Tom for the dermatologist also, and Alex for the orthopedist. The dermatologist is selected by majority vote. Note that the second semester vote was only between the dermatologist and the orthopedist because the students had already expressed a preference in the first semester election for the gynecologist.

The mythical student body never had the opportunity to vote between a gynecologist and an orthopedist. What would have happened if they had? Jane would have voted for the gynecologist, Tom for the orthopedist and Alex for the orthopedist. The orthopedist would have won! Thus, in many cases, getting an issue on or off an agenda (or its position on the agenda) of a sponsoring agency is *more significant* than the intrinsic worthiness of the project.

Markets, as mentioned previously in this chapter, cannot produce pure public goods and tend to under-produce goods with significant social benefits. Never fear, minimalists with respect to government spending would say. The political process has a built-in bias toward over-production of these goods!

In cases where there is not a transfer of income from one group in society to another, majority rule will tend, in the absence of a strong prohibition against spending, to provide enormous amounts of collective goods. An example of this may be seen in the case of married couples. New husbands often comment on how as bachelors they lived in relative comfort with Salvation Army furniture. These men claim, on the basis of such experience, that meaningful life is possible without matching towels and fancy tablewear. Less frequently mentioned are the cases in which new brides find themselves with state of the art stereo equipment and sports cars. The point is that prior to marriage neither had these possessions. Rather, they each respectively spent their incomes on highly individual things like clothes and trips. But if the family *has* to have the latest in high tech stereo equipment, which both enjoy (but clearly he more then she), the family also *has to have* fancy tablewear, which both enjoy (but clearly she more than he). This is a case of the expansion of collective goods whenever decisions are made by groups.

In sixth grade civics class the effect described above is called log-rolling. As a consequence of log-rolling, no one is relatively better or worse off from the supply of these goods. Log-rolling, however, typically requires a representative to vote for approval against his or her own preferences in the expectation that the favor will be returned. Thus, the subsequent general expansion of these goods may make both absolutely worse off.

9

HOW PRESSURE GROUPS APPLY THE HEAT

A criterion by which any group decides to provide itself with goods and services collectively was outlined in the previous chapter. Collective provision hinged, in Chapter 8, on whether the market failed to produce the desired good or service or, alternatively, on the existence of significant social benefits. The authors are willing to stand on the logic of such a rule. Admittedly, however, what ought to be, seldom is. And, therefore, the present chapter is an attempt to explain how not-for-profit firms sometimes get involved in the production of seemingly unlikely goods and services.

Why, for example, do communities have fleets of school buses but no mass transportation system? Why do hospitals provide, in some cases, evening meals for the fathers of newborns but not a bite for the spouse keeping virgil with the critically ill? It is "all politics." However, an understanding of the formation and operation of pressure groups is one way to get a handle on the direction in which not-for-profit firms evolve. Pressure groups apply the political heat to the sponsors and the constituency of not-for-profit firms in order to obtain those regulations, goods and services which serve their particular interests.

The terms "pressure group," "special interest group," and "public interest group" are used interchangeably. They may be thought of as the institutional manifestation of the active promotion of economic interests. That means they are groups trying to get others to buy and pay for goodies that they want. Either these groups cannot purchase these products in the profit-seeking sector or merely do not want to pay personally for them. In addition, they may gain employment opportunities or cheap inputs for their businesses if the product is produced collectively. Sometimes pressure groups will organize to get rid of "bads," such as pollution and crime. The Sierra Club, the Chamber of Commerce, the American Farm Bureau, and the American Education Association, and the American Medical Association are all public interest groups.

The term "public interest" is a smoke screen. There is no public interest in the sense of something being in the interest of the whole public. There are only particular interests. Can you define the public interest? If it is impossible to define the public interest, it becomes impossible to determine the extent to which the activity of a particular interest group or pressure group either helps or hinders progress toward the "general welfare."

Views of Public Interest Groups

Some see social reform growing out of man's natural inclination to association. They view public interest groups as being rather beneficial to society. When there is a need for a pressure group, one forms. Because a number of pressure groups form, these groups tend to counterbalance one another, ensuring that one group does not receive all the benefits.

Others contend that, when rational self-interested individuals realize that they have interests in common, and that they will benefit from collective action, they will develop into an organized interest group. Believers of this approach view society like a collective bargaining session. In other words, society can be divided into major sectors of interest and some authority must balance off the interests of one group against those of another.

Finally (and much more to the point in our view), in the public choice approach to interest groups, a pressure group acts to advance the interest of the group's members. However, when the pressure group begins to organize or to win benefits for its members, it is difficult to get members to pay up voluntarily. Pressure groups then actually are providing a collective good to their members and thus have problems with individuals who wish to receive the benefits without paying their dues. These individuals are called *"free riders."*

Characteristics of Pressure Groups

Some people derive benefits from pressure groups. But, strangely, whether or not a pressure group forms does not depend on the size of the anticipated benefits. Rather it depends on how the benefits will be distributed within the group and the way the costs of pressure group activity are assigned.

For example, assume that a group of students on a campus form a pressure group. It is likely that the aim of the group will be to get student fees to support a ski club, for example, which will yield a lot of benefits for athletic types, or some other clearly identifiable subset of students. It is less likely that a group of students will form to press for an efficient library reserve system that could possibly save a few dollars a year for all students who now purchase short but required paperbacks. It just is not worth anyone's time to organize and push for something which will yield such a small pay-off for the organizer. However, if you love to ski, the benefits to you personally of getting the school to invest in the ski club are considerable. The sum of the total benefits to all individuals at the college may be greater in the case of a good reserve system, but the benefits are distributed in such a way that the preconditions for such a group to get started do not exist.

The free rider problem is not so much a problem in the case of small pressure groups. Therefore, small pressure groups have less difficulty in organizing. At times, some members would be better off if a collective good was provided, even if they had to pay the entire cost themselves. And so, in some very small groups where each member gets a substantial portion of the total gain, the collective good is often provided by the voluntary action of members of the group. In addition, small groups which meet face-to-face can often use social sanctions as a means to coerce their members into supporting group goals.

How does one get a parent to be den leader for the cub scouts? If you have a seven year old and your child plus nine of his friends want to be cub scouts, you might under duress agree to serve. You personally will realize a large share of the benefits, approximately 1/9th, and, in addition, you may be able, after you serve for a year, to exert social pressure on the other "free rider" parents.

How to Avoid Extinction

Survival of a pressure group depends on getting members to pay up. Two techniques may be used to accomplish this. First, the pressure group may develop a legal mechanism which allows its members to coerce themselves into paying for the collective good. Unions fight or advantages for certain groups of people. It would be ideal to reap the benefits of union activity without being a member. But, alas, many jobs are not available to you unless you join up and pay dues.

Sometimes, pressure groups resort to funding their activities by providing, in addition to the collective good, some divisible individual good. For example, the American Automobile Association, which lobbies for better highways, provides some divisible goods like emergency road and routing services. Eventually, however, the pressure group is subject to competition from organizations willing to provide the same divisible benefits but at a lower cost. For example, the AMOCO Automobile Club might provide emergency services and routing at a slightly lower fee than the American Automobile Association (AAA) but with no lobbying service.

Pressure groups may have their platforms ripped out from under them sometimes. An on-the-move politician may feel that he or she can make hay with the voters by championing the same causes as the pressure groups, and they champion the cause free of charge. Pressure groups often aid political entrepreneurs in discovering their profit opportunities more rapidly (in the sense of votes, not dollars!).

Pressure Group Reform

Pressure groups could be left as is or, if one insists on reform, handled in three alternate ways. First, they could have voting ministries in Congress to represent their interest. Second, the provisions of the Internal Revenue Code, affecting lobbying activity, could be changed. And, finally, all projects supported by public interest groups could be financed out of taxes that are levied on specific groups in the total population, although not necessarily on the same groups securing the benefits.

The problems of an assembly with ministries representing various interest groups is that legislators would not feasibly be able to trade off one interest in favor of another. The situation could exist where the degree of compromise necessary to a democracy might be unattainable. In other words, the minister would be judged exclusively in terms of one area which he or she represents.

A Minister of Education, for example, would have to vote affirmatively on every "pro-education" bill. He would be unable to vote negatively on inconsequential issues in return for the votes of other ministers when significant bills affecting education came to the floor. The only way he could win votes for education would be by voting affirmatively on all proposals vested in the interest of his or her coalition.

The second type of reform would result in reducing the amount of lobbying. The Internal Revenue Code could be amended to eliminate specialized mailing privileges and the tax deductibility of contributions for pressure groups. Deductible contributions account for approximately 40 percent of pressure group income. Some not-for-profit "charitable" firms must be careful not to give the impression that their primary function is to operate as disguised pressure groups for their donors.

The purpose of the third proposal, which may be too theoretical and farfetched for practice, is to set up a watchdog group to blow the cover on any project which did not in the long run yield benefits for those paying the costs.

For example, if a lobbying group were trying to get Congress to pass on aid to a particular country or on concessions to businessmen dealing with that country, funds to sponsor this program might be controlled through a special tax levied on the residents of one particular state, like Virginia. All the other states would be indifferent to the proposals and the lobbying group consisting of firms selling abroad would be egging on the Congress. The costs would be dumped on Virginia, but the representatives from Virginia would monitor the proceedings carefully. They would observe those representatives from other states who were shifting costs to their state. Then they would try to influence as many indifferent congressmen in an offsetting manner with threats of reprisal. This political process would produce a solution which might be better than general tax financing, where everybody would be hurt a little by helping the lobbying group but not enough to get hot enough to do something about it. In other words, if the whole price of a project is borne by one group there is a greater liklihood that the whole project will be better scrutinized.

Pressure groups will always exist. Their activities will be observed and evaluated over the counter or they will operate underground in the political process. Their activity should not be encouraged or discouraged. Ideally, but this is merely an opinion, they should operate on the outside rather than from a power base inside the not-for-profit organization. It is only by understanding how they operate that one can explain what goods and services not-for-profit organizations will sponsor.

10

TO TELL THE TRUTH: THE DEMAND FOR PUBLIC GOODS

When not-for-profit firms are producing private goods paid for by the user, the problems of estimating demand and marketing the product are essentially the same as those of a profit-seeking firm. However, in the case of a public good, estimating demand is very tricky. If one has to pay personally for the Public Good, consumers claim they can do without the product, hoping that someone else will provide it! On the other hand, if an agreement has been made to provide the good collectively, why not ask for more?

Estimation of Demand

The economic theory of demand is derived from the way in which economists view individual consumers. Economists believe individual consumers act with a purpose: they choose among alternatives in order to maximize their well-being. Economists develop models based on such individuals *not* to explain the behavior of single individuals (which is perhaps the task of psychologists) but rather to make predictions about how individuals as groups (in the aggregate) will act.

The market demand for a particular good or service is the aggregate of the demands of the various individuals who desire the good or service. Empirically estimating the demand for different items can be a valuable technique. Consider the case of a firm which wants to know what reaction to expect if it reduces price by twenty percent. Knowledge of the demand for it's product (i.e. knowledge of how individuals in the aggregate will react to changes in price) would be essential to the firm trying to make a rational pricing decision. Given a certain demand estimate the firm might expect total revenue to decrease as it reduces its price—under other conditions total revenue could increase with a price decrease. The important point to see is that empirical estimates of demand can be invaluable in providing the raw information for rational decisions.

Many not-for-profit firms and government agencies, however, run into trouble when estimating the demand for their goods and services—and with good reason. The demand for the good or service of a not-for-profit firm may be very *unlike* the demand for something produced by a profit-seeking firm. Consider the private good orange juice produced by numerous private, profit-seeking firms. Orange juice is a private good because an individual, like yourself, can purchase it and drink it *and* exclude anyone else from drinking the particular bottle you purchase. The demand for orange juice can be calculated by summing the demand all individuals have for orange juice. Recall that an individual's demand for orange juice is merely the different quantities he or she would purchase at different prices. One individual's demand for orange juice can be represented in Figure 10-1. This individual would buy three bottles *if* the price were $1.50 per bottle and four bottles *if* the price were $1.00 per bottle. This person is behaving according to the law of demand because as the price of orange juice decreases, the quantity demanded by the person increases.

DEMAND OF A SINGLE INDIVIDUAL FOR BOTTLES OF ORANGE JUICE

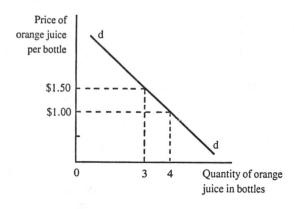

Figure 10-1

If we wanted to know the demand for orange juice for the entire community of which the person above was just one member, we could inquire of each and every community member the quantities of orange juice he or she would purchase at various prices. By adding up the total amount which would be purchased by all consumers at $1.50 (and plotting that) and then adding up the total amount which would be purchased at $1.00 (and plotting that) and so on, we could empirically estimate a demand curve like the one in Figure 10-2. This curve would indicate the total number of bottles of orange juice which would be purchased at different prices—it includes at $1.50 the three bottles our individual above would purchase *and* all other bottles purchased by other community members at the $1.50 price. The demand curve in Figure 10-2 is just the horizontal summation of all the individual demand curves like the one in Figure 1. But remember that orange juice is a private good—if you drink it, it's gone and no one else can use it.

Many goods (and services) produced by not-for-profit firms are not private goods, however. Some of them are public

MARKET DEMAND FOR ORANGE JUICE

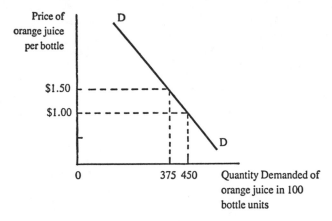

Figure 10-2

goods—goods which everyone (or everybody in a particular group) can receive benefits from at the same time. Increases in environmental quality is an example of a public good—if the air in a particular locale is cleaned up, everyone living in the area is better off simultaneously. No individual living in the area can be excluded from the benefits of the now cleaner air. But what is the demand for cleaner air? Since it is a public good can its demand be estimated using the technique outlined above for private goods? Consider the individual we interviewed above concerning orange juice purchases. Suppose we visit this same individual again and ask what quantities of air purification he or she would purchase at various prices. This is a distinctly *different* situation than asking about orange juice purchases. The individual knows that he or she alone will receive the benefits of any orange juice purchased but if air purification services are purchased everyone else in the community will receive the benefits from the individual's purchase. How can you exclude someone from breathing "your" clean air?

There is the possibility that the individual when questioned about how much air purification he or she would buy would engage in one of two behaviors. First, the individual could reason that since everyone in the community is going to receive the benefits of any purchase (resulting in purer air), he or she would only like to purchase a part of the air purification services. The individual might expect others to contribute a part of the expense too, so that all could benefit from the cleaner air. Economists call this "strategic behavior" and it is common to all situations involving public goods. How would this affect the individual demand curve estimate for air purification services? If air purification services had been a private good (such as an air purifier for an individual house) the individual's demand might have been d_2d_2 in Figure 10-3. But, since air purification services benefit the whole community (i.e. are a public good), the individual consumer chooses to purchase less at every price (as shown by demand curve d_1d_1) and hopes others will contribute to the public good. This is strategic behavior in the sense that the individual's decision is affected by what he or she

DEMAND OF A SINGLE INDIVIDUAL FOR AIR PURIFICATION SERVICES

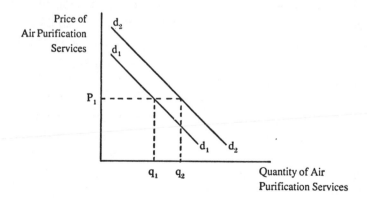

Figure 10-3

feels others will do. Note that in purchasing the private good (orange juice) the individual has no reason to care what quantity others will purchase or at what price those units will be purchased. The strategic behavior is the result of the public goods characteristic of the air purification services. No such behavior would be expected when estimating the demand for a private good.

The second, and more drastic, behavior which can be expected of individuals in public goods demand situations is free riding. Free riding is actually the polar case of strategic behavior; if the individual feels that others will buy the air purification services and he or she can receive the benefits without making any contribution to the purchase, the individual may have *no demand*. That is, the individual is unwilling to buy any air purification services at any price because of the knowledge (presumption) that others will supply it. It would be quite possible (and rational) for each member of the community to free ride by reporting that he or she has no demand for air purification services. Thus we might aggregate these perceived preferences and conclude that there is no market demand for air purification services.

What is the appropriate measure of the market demand for a good or service with public characteristics? How could it be calculated? Let's assume there are only two individuals in the community we are examining, Mr. A and Ms. B. Figure 10-4 shows the individual demands of A and B (labelled d_a and d_b) *if* we could convince A and B to tell us their true preferences (in the absence of any strategic behavior or free riding). To find the market demand for air purification services we would *vertically* sum the curves d_a and d_b. For instance, A would be willing to purchase 3 units at a price of $1.00 and B would be willing to purchase 3 units at $2.00. The total value to the community of 3 units of air purification would then be $2.00 plus $1.00 (what Mr. A is willing to pay *plus* what Ms. B is willing to pay) or

INDIVIDUAL AND MARKET DEMAND FOR AIR PURIFICATION SERVICES

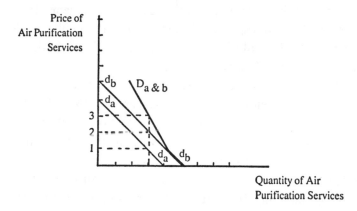

Figure 10-4

$3.00. The difficulty of doing this empirically lies in the impracticality of obtaining truthful estimates from individuals of their valuations of public goods. Any simple survey of the populace asking the number of units which would be purchased at various prices would always be biased by strategic behavior.

Marketing the Output of Not-for-Profit Firms

Recall that not-for-profit firms are normally established to serve the goals of a large number of individuals. These not-for-profit firms are not judged on the basis of a profit and loss statement but on the perception of their effectiveness in their efforts to provide the intended good or service. Whether the not-for-profit firm provides what is essentially a private good or what is essentially a public good, revenue or income is important to the organization. This revenue determines the level of services or goods which the organization can provide. In a profit-seeking institution, the revenue-producing function is called marketing.

The actual selling of the product or service in these firms often takes the priority position in administrative assignments. In the not-for-profit firm, especially in the provision of public goods, the product being sold is largely intangible. The benefits are indirect and quite often rather vague.

Not-for-profit institutions such as universities or hospitals, which provide essentially private goods, are able to market their goods or services easily. One might question whether these institutions should market their service at all, the argument being that marketing merely increases the cost to the users of the service. Why should a hospital, for instance, market its services when the marketing function merely serves to increase the cost to the patients of the hospital?

Marketing, however, both for not-for-profit and for profit-seeking institutions is best thought of as not merely advertising. If marketing meant only advertising, then it would be quite true that many not-for-profit firms and many profit-seeking firms might quite rationally choose not to advertise. Marketing, however, can be thought of as merely the facilitating of exchange relationships. In the case of a hospital, marketing would mean the designing, the communicating about, and finally the delivery of products and services that satisfy the consumer's needs and wants. When marketing is thought of in this fashion, it can be seen to benefit not only the not-for-profit hospital, but also the customers of that hospital.

By facilitating an exchange or trade, both parties to the exchange, the hospital and the hospital's customers, benefit from the exchange. Many hospitals engage in patient education classes, pre-admission visits for scheduled patients, and tours of new facilities. Other health care facilities offer glaucoma and high blood pressure tests as a means of communicating with the public. All of these activities could be seen as marketing on the part of the non-profit hospital.

It has been suggested by some that these marketing techniques are meant to manipulate consumers in order to increase demand for the goods and services which the hospital provides. Because there are many hospitals, however, and many hospitals find themselves in competition with other hospitals in a local area, little manipulation is actually possible on the part of a single hospital. These marketing techniques, like those used by profit-seeking companies in competitive situations, actually benefit not only the firm but also the consumer.

Other not-for-profit firms provide what are largely public goods. Consider the case of a community or "educational" television station. These television stations available in many local communities normally operate on the UHF band which covers the television spectrum of Channel 14 and above. These television stations are organized as not-for-profit corporations and provide a service which is largely a public good. The transmissions of the station are largely a public good because the station has no possibility of excluding any individuals with television sets from receiving and enjoying the signal.

Once an individual is an owner of a television set, there is no way at present to exclude him from the viewing population of the educational television station. Marketing for the educational television station, or for other non-profit firms which also provide public goods like libraries and museums, is a much more delicate matter than marketing for non-profit corporations which provide largely private goods.

The product being sold by the educational television station is quite intangible and the benefits of a "membership" in the educational television station are clearly indirect and certainly very vague. A hallmark, however, of every successful educational television station and likewise of every successful library or museum, is a well organized and well run marketing department.

The ability to generate revenue successfully and continuously over a long period of time ensures the survival of these not-for-profit institutions. The non-profit "name tag" may actually be the blind spot that keeps many organizations from doing what they must do to achieve their goals. Because many not-for-profit firms, like educational television stations or libraries, do not like to be thought of as "selling" their product or service, these firms show little interest in the subject of marketing. It is after all awkward for a firm that derives a large percentage of its revenue from a sponsoring organization, to admit that clients are not beating their doors down trying to get what they provide.

Perhaps these firms which supply largely a public good, however, make a major error in equating marketing with selling. Marketing must be though of as the broader activity of adapting the organization to a rapidly changing environment and assisting the organization to grow to its potential. It may be the case that marketing benefits both the non-profit organization and its constituents, as potential users become aware of their alternatives and seek the services of those not-for-profit firms that best suit their needs.

PART IV

THE
ORGANIZATION

11

ORGANIZATIONAL FRAMEWORK

A powerful mural by Clemente Orosco hangs in the foyer of the city hall of Guadalajara in Jalisco, Mexico. Beside the flaming figure of Hidalgo, the patron of Mexican independence, is the body of a man with a pole and typewriter for his head. Such was Orosco's image of a bureaucrat. Perhaps, if he were painting in the seventies rather than in the twenties, he would paint in a computer or a key puncher. Most of us go to great lengths to avoid dealing with a bureaucracy. Thus, the image of the non-responsive, inefficient and slow bureaucrat is perpetuated. The word bureaucracy is often not used carefully. In current usage it refers either to a large organization or one that is somehow not responsive to those who wish to avail themselves of its services. Therefore the word and certainly the feeling conjured up by the word are often appropiate to not-for-profit firms. The problem, however, is not necessarily one of bigness. The small town marriage license bureau that closes at five every night and remains closed on Saturdays is certainly not big!

Actually there are ways to get such firms to respond, but not always in the desired direction and not necessarily through the channels that one would expect to use in dealing with the firm. The not-for-profit firm, defined as an organization in which the owners do not necessarily receive the difference of revenue minus cost is a special case of bureaucracy. Furthermore, some part of the annual budget of the organization is derived from something other than the sale of final output. In addition, the customer cannot switch his patronage without moving or changing his memebership in some way.

The following chart presents the three basic groups that the head of a not-for-profit firm must deal with. The head of an educational institution is generally referred to as an administrator, while other not-for-profit firms are led by a head, chief or director. We will use the term administrator to denote all of the above. An administrator, then, is one who has the responsibility of administrating an identifiable budget in a not-for-profit firm.

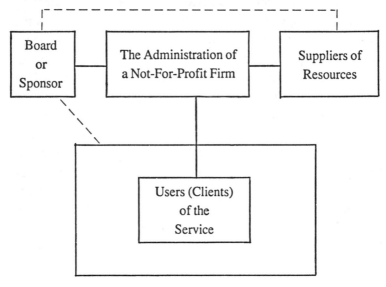

Figure 11-1

Faculty and students at many universities often joke that the president is never around except during graduation and whenever parents and alumni are on campus. Is there any case of a university president being fired by the students? Admittedly, the administrator of a not-for-profit firm often directs his or her energy outside the organization. He or she is dominated by relationships with the sponsors of the organization. The sponsor of the organization is the group of officers responsible for reviewing and appropriating the budget.

The type of sponsor may vary from one firm to another. In a private university, the president will allocate most of his efforts toward parents, alumni and the Board of Trustees. In a state university, the president will allocate less time to these groups and proportionally more to the state legislature. A division director or agency head acts similarly. An effective administrator is one who handles these relationships well. Agency clients and students seem to reluctantly resign themselves to this. Inexperienced employees are also frustrated by the failure of top level administrators to recognize a job well-done. On the other hand, lower level bureaucrats (i.e. faculty, case workers, desk officers) drive administrators wild complaining about their myopic concerns like parking and supplies and fail to notice when the head has just pulled down a large budget appropriation.

The sponsor, often an elected representative or an appointed board member, is on the receiving end of this attention from the chief administrator. However, the sponsor is often not in a position to evaluate whatever information the administrator provides. Therefore, the sponsor passively approves the suggestions of the administrators. For example, in government programs, a politician knows what types of projects he wants to support and how far he wants to go in supporting them. But seldom is it politically worth his time and effort to become an expert in the area of a particular not-for-profit firm. And, because the firm is in all probability a monopoly supplier of the service, accurate comparison data are not available for him or her to make an informed judgment on matters of cost per unit of output or efficient combination of resources used to produce the product.

Boards of private institutions may also be rather passive. Some, as in the case of credit unions and school boards, are individuals doing the job on a volunteer unpaid basis. Their motivation is at times unclear. They may be using it as a community service project to put on their job inventory sheet as a basis for promotion in their regular job. They may be businessmen who are using the exposure as a form of free advertising (e.g. bankers and real estate agents commonly engage in this practice). Or they may be persons with a certain amount of free time who are using the opportunity for personal gratification. These latter types will generally spend enormous amounts of time and effort in reviewing the operations of the agency. They are potentially the most threatening to the administrator, but, if they do not have some personal ax to grind, they can operate as an effective check on the organization.

In terms of control, the most effective group of sponsors are those that have something to gain by efficiency and effectiveness in the organization. For example, the interests of alumni and parents in educational institutions are closely tied with the users of the agency. We are not indicating that this type of sponsor is always desirable. Parents may wish, for example, to control the schools that their children attend but for which the community, as a whole, pays. Understandably, parents will press for the highest quality and range of programs.

The complexity of relationships within the not-for-profit firm is further highlighted by suppliers of inputs to the firm. Generally, these inputs or resources are hired on a competitive basis at market prices. Sometimes, however, the not-for-profit firm is a monopoly buyer of these resources. In some communities only one agency is hiring nurses, teachers, firemen, police and welfare workers. The agency could use this opportunity to pay lower wages but generally does not. In fact, the number of people willing and waiting to be called to these jobs exceeds the number of vacancies. This indicates that they are not underpaid with respect to alternative opportunities in the community.

Individuals who work for these agencies often find it in their best interest to organize to exert pressure on the agency indirectly through the sponsors. This is possible for two reasons. First of all, the conditions exist for an effecive interest group of resource suppliers to bring pressure on the sponsors of the agency. Secondly, the sponsors, wishing to be reelected, are responsive to organized interest groups. Contracts and jobs are often awarded with the implicit or explicit intervention of the sponsor.

Further complicating the picture are the two groups of customers. These consist of the larger population supporting the firm and the clients who directly utilize the services of the firm. In general, the greater the revenue derived directly from the client relative to the total budget of the firm the more responsive the organization is to clients. This relationship is discussed in Chapter 13.

It might be suggestd that the awkward relationships outlined above for not-for-profit firms are characteristic of all firms. One must not forget, however, that the critical characteristic of the firm under discussion in this book is that part of the agency's revenue is not derived from the direct sale of output to customers. This basic institutional difference results in an organizational framework that appears to be similar to a profit-seeking firm but is, in reality, not as well-focused. Efforts to dazzle the board of directors, hire politically, and ignore customers are aberrations in the profit-seeking firm. They often constitute rational behavior and are the norm in a not-for-profit situation.

Economists deal both with the firm as a micro unit as well as with the collection of firms that constitute an industry. In conclusion we must therefore say something about the ''not-for-profit industry'' or the long term effects of a group of not-for-profit firms. In this "industry" if just one administrator of a public not-for-profit firm decides to maximize his or her budget by entering into new areas, then all the rest in the "industry" will follow. In perfect competition if all corporations are becoming conglomerates it is possible for one firm to specialize and concentrate on producing one product better or cheaper and thus maintain a return of profit equal to or better than his competitors. On the other hand, in the public not-for-profit environment if one firm chooses to be a conglomerate it will behoove the rest to move in that direction or they will most likely experience a loss in their budget. Thus we hear laments about needless duplication of medical facilities and educational departments. Such duplication is inevitable. However, in Chapter 19 we will suggest that attempts to "streamline" the industry may be counterproductive.

12

OUTPUT DECISIONS: TOO MUCH OF

A GOOD THING

One morning on the Phil Donohue Show, Senator Edward Kennedy outlined his program for socialized medicine. This well-prepared and articulated individual expounded what he sincerely believes, perhaps correctly, to be a strongly felt need of his political constituency. In any case, a gentleman in the audience, who indentified himself as a Canadian physician, asked if the program had built-in controls to prevent overusage. The senator replied that such programs do tend to be overused at first but, once backed up demands are met, usage returns to acceptable levels.

The question of determining the proper levels of output in a not-for-profit firm is an economic problem of major importance. It must be dealt with for any program partially or totally funded through a budget derived from some source other than the sale of output. Very little work has been done in this area. One would expect that free-market anti-socialist economists would be anxious to demonstrate the overallocation that results when users pay a price less than the marginal cost.

The dearth of work in this area is due, perhaps, to a fear of using economic tools where they are not appropriate. Ludwig Von Mises in *Bureaucracy* cautions that bureaucratic management is management of affairs which cannot be checked by economic calculation. He suggests that what appear to be bureaucratic inefficiencies may well be the inevitable result of institutional conditions. Unfortunately, Von Mises states, there may not be another alternative for provision of these goods or services. Like Patrick Henry, he recommends eternal vigilance over the working of the bureaucracy. In addition, he suggests that the bureaucracy operate under a rule rather than by the discretion of administrators.

In spite of such warnings, it is likely that at least a few trained in microeconomics succumbed. The temptation of trying to demonstrate the wastes of not-for-profit production graciously adjusting for social benefits, of course, is irresistible. Either the few who tried gave up because the results fail to support their normative stance or because of theoretical complexity. The latter reason is certainly plausible to any who have tried to hack their way through the thicket.

COSTS

What determines the quantity of goods and services that any firm offers? One of the major factors is the cost of producing these goods and services. Hence cost is a fundamental concept in economics. Not only is it the basis for determining the amount of output, but it is important in any decision among several alternatives. Whenever a decision is made, an economist thinks of the cost of the decision in terms of the opportunity cost. In other words, a dollar spent on anything must be compared with what could be gained if it were spent on another thing. It is not trivial to question if too many resources (in terms of their opportunity cost) are being allocated to health care or some other such service in a particular community.

Generally, in the profit seeking sector, economists suggest that resources are properly allocated through the price mechanism. If individuals desire health care in a private market, for example, the price they are willing to pay for it is a reflection of the desire. Given competition, firms will produce an amount of that service up to the point where the extra or marginal cost of producing the product is equal to the price. This assumes, of course, that the producer is bearing all the cost of producing the product, including social costs such as pollution. Furthermore, it assumes that there is no reason to subsidize an individual to consume more of the product than he wishes to spend voluntarily for the product.

Because the price or the fee that a user of the output of a not-for-profit firm pays is generally less than full cost, economic theory alone cannot determine what is the "correct" amount. Consequently, opportunity costs are particularly important in the case of not-for-profit firms. Given some fixed budget, the decision to provide one good must be at the expense of another. In calculating the opportunity cost of any decision, economists include both explicit and implicit costs.

Explicit costs are obvious, out-of-pocket expenditures such as cash outlays required to obtain goods or services (e.g. wages paid for work done, interest paid to bondholders for the loan of their money, payments made to suppliers for raw materials). Implicit costs associated with any decision are more difficult to identify because they do not involve cash expenditures. A church that uses its social hall on weekday afternoons for scouting rather than renting it out to other religious groups for religious education is incurring an important implicit cost for scouting.

Total cost to an economist is the full cost (the sum of explicit and implicit costs) of any decision. Imagine that two fraternities wish to finance their rush activities. One fraternity has the funds available in the chapter to do so, and the other must borrow the funds with interest from their national organization to conduct the activities. Whose costs are higher? It is not clear. An economist would say the firm with the money on hand should consider as costs what they would have earned by keeping the money in the next best alternative (such as a savings account). Therefore, the total cost of the rush activities is the sum of the explicit costs paid out by the fraternity and the implicit costs of foregone interest that would have been paid on existing funds.

Marginal Cost and Diminishing Returns

While total cost is the full cost (explicit and implicit) involved in any decision, marginal cost is the cost of producing only one additional unit of a good or service. Marginal cost is the change in total cost brought about by a one-unit change in output. The marginal cost of educating the 2001st student at a university would be the difference between the total cost of educating 2000 students and the total cost of educating 2001 students. The marginal or additional cost of successive units of any product or service may be constant, increasing, or decreasing according to the particular situation. One characteristic of marginal cost is certain, however, as more and more units of a good are produced in the short run (a period of time during which a firm cannot change the size of its plant), the marginal cost will begin to rise at some point. This is the same as saying that marginal cost curves will have the U shape shown in Figure 12-1.

As more and more students are educated on a single campus, the marginal cost (change in total cost resulting from the production of one additional unit) of educating students falls in the not-for-profit firm. It is plausible that two students could be educated with only a few more total resources than one, thus, marginal costs are reduced. But does the marginal cost continue declining forever as more and more units are produced? No.

The economist has a term for why marginal cost must sooner or later begin to rise: the law of diminishing returns. This law states that as more and more units of a variable factor (say, teachers, paper, classes, etc.) are combined with fixed amounts of other resources (say, classrooms, dormitories, etc.), output per unit of input declines or cost per unit of service will eventually rise. Thus carrying the enrollment beyond point A in the Figure 12-1 would mean each additional student adds more and more to marginal costs.

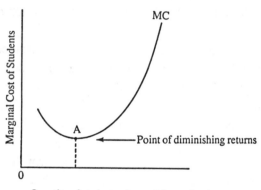

Figure 12-1

Marginal Analysis

It is hypothesized here that the traditional tools of marginal cost and marginal revenue can be used to analyze the output decision making of a not-for-profit organization. The exposition presented here is based on the work of William Niskanen, who has developed a theory of output determination in the not-for-profit firm in *Bureaucracy and Representative Government*.

The profit-seeking firm produces where marginal revenue equals marginal cost. Profits are maximized at this point if the marginal cost approaches this point from values less than marginal revenue. Given a perfectly elastic demand curve, price is also equal to marginal revenue. An output where price is equal to marginal cost is defined as the correct allocation of resources because the marginal valuation (price) of the consumer is neither greater nor less than the marginal opportunity cost of the resources in the production of some other good or service. Generally, a monopoly will charge a higher price and produce a lower level of output. Under what conditions will a not-for-profit firm produce more, less, or that precise amount of output defined by the marginal valuation being equal to the marginal cost?

The administrator of a not-for-profit firm is assumed to be a budget maximizer. The financing of such a firm is derived from the sale of the service and/or the budget approved by the sponsoring organization. The efforts of the administrator and indeed the responsiveness of the organization will accordingly be focused at the margin on which of these two groups will contribute most to the total revenue of the firm. The *budget output function* represents the maximum budget that the sponsoring organization is willing to grant the firm for a specific expected level of output. The customer or client preference for the service of the not-for-profit firm is the *price output relationship* of a normal demand curve. The sum of the budget-output function and the revenue derived from the price-output functions represents the total budget of the firm.

The cost of producing a certain level of output is related, of course, to the cost output function. There is no reason to believe that this curve is any different from the cost output function of a profit-making firm. It is true that often the not-for-profit firm is in a monopsonistic (monopoly buyer) situation. In many towns, who but the school corporation buys the services of fifth grade teachers? Often, however, the not-for-profit firm does not exploit this advantage.

The not-for-profit firm does not try to maximize the difference between revenue and costs. It tries to maximize the budget subject to its revenue being at least equal or greater than costs. Figures 12-2, 12-3 and 12-4 assume that a sponsor fully financing the not-for-profit firm will increase the budget with respect to output up to some level. The sponsor will not pay more than a given amount for any additional output. Three possibilities result when all the revenue is derived from a sponsoring organization:

1. The budget that the sponsoring organization is willing to grant is maximized at a level of output at which the not-for-profit firm will not produce because it cannot cover costs. Therefore, it produces at the breakeven point. Because the administrator is a budget maximizer, the output level will be at point B rather than point A in Figure 12-2.

2. The budget that the sponsoring organization is willing to grant is maximized at a level of output where total costs are less than the budget. Therefore, given Figure 12-3, the firm produces at point A.

3. The budget that the sponsoring organization is willing to grant is at one point tangent at the total cost curve but never above it. Therefore, given Figure 12-4, the firm produces at Point 0.

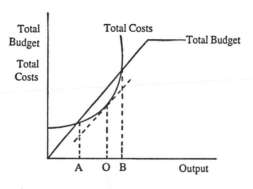

Figure 12-2

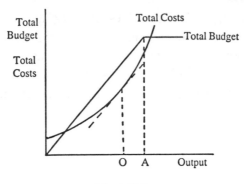

Figure 12-3

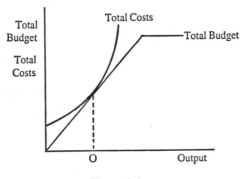

Figure 12-4

In the first and second case more than the socially optimum level of output is produced. The socially optimum level of output is defined as that level of output where the marginal cost to society of producing the last unit is equal to the marginal value of the product to society, expressed by what people are willing to pay for the product. Graphically this is where the slope of the budget output function is equal to the price output relationship. This is point 0 in Figures 12-2, 12-3 and 12-4.

In Figure 12-3, however, there is reason for additional concern because the not-for-profit firm will absorb the residual between the amount budgeted and total cost. The total amount budgeted will be spent, which is, of course, a cardinal rule of a bureaucrat. There is, after all, no reason for the not-for-profit firm to reveal its true cost structure to the sponsoring organization.

The case presented in Figure 12-4 is ideal. The problem, of course, is that it depends on a happy coincidence, that is the sponsoring organization's refusal to reveal its preferences until the not-for-profit firm reveals its true costs.

If any market, real or synthetic, existed, it would be possible to ensure a better allocation of resources. Not-for-profit organizations producing an output for a price, determined in competition with profit-seeking or other not-for-profit firms, would produce where marginal cost equals marginal revenue and with no residual. After all, in equilibrium, the competitive process results in nothing except normal profits for each profit-seeking firm.

In conclusion, it seems that the failure to deal with output decision making in the not-for-profit firm may be related to the fact that the theoretical conclusion does not *a priori* suggest unambiguously either an over- or under-allocation of resources. The problem is one of a demand or cost revealing process. The theoretical complexity of the problem is enormous but could be very fruitful if approached through game theory. Game theory is an attempt to outline all possible outcomes when two or more parties choose interdependent risky alternatives. Ultimately, however, the problem of successful surveillance and monitoring depends on a cost revealing process which necessitates creating quasi-competitive conditions.

Why worry about producing too much of a good thing? Because no society, at this point in time, can afford the best possible education, health care, etc. for each of its members. Therefore, more of one good thing means less of another. It is legitimate for the sponsors of not-for-profit firms to question what might be the over-allocation of funds to the production of less desirable goods and services. The sponsors cannot depend on the firm itself to warn that the current level of output is enough.

13

THE CUSTOMER: IS HE OR SHE

ALWAYS WRONG?

In a book of short chapters, this will be one of the shortest. It is an attempt to demonstrate the status of the client in a not-for-profit firm. The position of clients in the firm, rather than any other factor, gives rise to the feeling of helplessness that characterize the sick patient waiting for a nurse, the student standing in a long line for registration, as well as the welfare client visiting one office after another seeking a special voucher.

The unresponsiveness of bureaucracy, assumed to be the inevitable consequence of bigness, is due rather to the institutional characteristics of not-for-profit firms. McDonald's and Bell Telephone (usually thought to be responsive organizations) are bigger than most city and some state governments. Neither does the unresponsiveness result from the fact that most not-for-profit firms are dealing, not with hamburgers or telephone service, but with outputs that are difficult to measure. Doctors, lawyers and New York Life also engage in outputs that are not easily measured.

It is naive to assume that the customer is never cheated in the profit-seeking sector. Goods often fall apart, home improvement and service contracts are not honored, and product information is sometimes misleading, if not false. But as consumers we can learn to adapt to this by changing products, being more shrewd in negotiating contracts, or in the extreme, learning how to provide these goods and services for ourselves.

But as the saying goes, you can't fight city hall. The taxpayer must take what he gets, and he will pay for it whether he uses the service or not. Sometimes, in a round about way, the product of a not-for-profit firm seems like a bargain. Ice skating for one dollar at the city rink or bingo for three dollars at the church appear to be a better bargain than a movie for three dollars and fifty cents at the mall. It is not that you necessarily prefer skating and bingo, rather it is the case that you have already indirectly forked out the rent for the rink and the church hall. So why not use it?

Responsiveness to the customer is the characteristic most appealing about a profit-seeking firm. But it is interesting to note that this responsiveness is neither of a "give them what they want" nature nor of a "take it or leave it" nature. Rather, a profit-seeking firm makes policy decisions that it hopes will result in profit for itself. They do not permit the customers to determine policy. A good Italian restaurant does not permit its customers to plan the menu. McDonald's will not serve mashed potatoes and corned beef to even its best customers. A mistake, in the opinion of the authors, is often made when a not-for-profit firm attempts to be customer oriented. These firms actually allow the customer (who is really only a user) to make administrative policy. The customer, in our view, has no right except the right to be well served.

The key to the effective provision of goods and services in the not-for-profit firm is the fact that "you only get what you pay for directly." Not-for-profit firms producing a private good depend on customers. And customers will not patronize any organization that does not provide them with what they freely pay for. Of course, some not-for-profit organizations are so well endowed that they can pay customers to use their service! Scholarships are a case in point.

User Fees

User charges are those receipts designed to cover the full cost of providing a particular service of a not-for-profit firm. *User fees* are charges upon direct users of facilites and services of not-for-profit firms but are not designed to cover the full cost of providing that service. This is often the case with fees for institutions of higher education, school lunch sales, public buses and hospitals.

In Chapter 12, we noted that the efficient allocation of resources requires that price be set equal to marginal cost. In a competitive market, if price falls below marginal cost, some producers will leave the market and price will increase to provide a return to the private producer adequate to cover his total costs.

The revenue derived from user fees is often not expected to be a major source of revenue to a not-for-profit firm. In fact there is generally some concern that lower income people who are members of the sponsoring organizations will be priced out of using the service. This is a serious problem because individuals who are actually being "taxed" to provide the product are unable to use it.

At this point it should be mentioned that, rightly or wrongly, large groups of individuals are excluded from prestigious universities and recreational facilities that they pay for indirectly but cannot afford to pay for directly. For example, an individual family may be paying $500 on their home in property taxes. About 50 of these dollars could be used to pay the interest on bonds or to maintain the grounds of a public golf course. A user fee for each round of golf may be $5.00, plus caddying expenses. Many families in the community may not be able to play golf because of the user fee. Yet they are subsidizing others to do so. The $5.00 fee, although quite reasonable, is an excellent way of allocating the use of the course particularly on weekends but it may act to discourage those with low incomes from ever playing.

Sometimes individuals who subsidize public goods are excluded on other than an economic basis. State universities may, for example, discriminate among applicants on the basis of test scores. Recreation facilities often discriminate against the handicapped. Such is the problem with collectively provided goods. The solution, however, is not in providing universities for the nonacademically prepared and special recreational facilities for all. The society that can provide all things for all people does not exist. If it did, it would not need to consider economic efficiency.

Quite aside from any considerations of equity, user fees are instituted when congestion occurs to allocate the good or service. To even out use, a municipal park may charge a fee on weekends but have free admission on weekdays. Similarly, on-street parking in business districts is typically not metered during after-business hours and on holidays because after-hours parking is not as scarce as parking is during business hours. These fees do yield revenue but the manager of a not-for-profit firm is often discouraged from using them. Taxpayers who play tennis on city courts get very hot and bothered, and feel they are being persecuted when they have to pay to play. But then they like even less waiting several hours to play or being turned away at the gate.

User fees are often discussed in connection with the *benefit principle of taxation,* which means that each person should pay his or her share of a collectively provided good proportionally to the extent that he or she uses the good. When spillovers or externalities are minimal and the beneficiaries are easily identified, the benefit principle has considerable appeal. Sunday school fees can be charged to parents rather than the whole congregation. When the collectively provided good has large spillovers or externalities, however, taxation on the benefit principle is difficult because it is impossible to observe who benefits and by what amount in order to figure out charges. Police protection, national defense and unions are examples of firms in which it would be very difficult to isolate the extent to which each individual benefits. In one sense all benefit equally, but this may not be the fact. For example, it may be the less motivated workers that stand to gain the most from unionization. Similar cases may be made for police protection and national security.

Many not-for-profit firms are organized primarily to sell services directly to citizens. This is the case with public not-for-profit firms called public enterprises such as the Tennessee Valley Authority, municipally owned water and electric departments, toll bridges and toll roads. It is also the case with private not-for-profit firms such as hospitals, nursing homes and some educational institutions. These operations are expected to be self-financing. Such firms are not expected to seek a profit and if they happen to make a profit it generally reverts into the general revenue of the sponsoring organization.

The statement that you get what you pay for directly implies that the larger the percentage of total revenue derived from user fees the more responsive that organization is to the client. In other words, institutions where students directly pay a significant percentage of the total revenue of the institution are generally student oriented. They tend towards smaller classes and more faculty-student contact than schools dependent on tax revenue, endowments and grants.

There is one important qualification to the rule that higher user fees means better customer service. Any not-for-profit firm given a monopoly charter from its sponsoring organization will have little incentive to be effective regardless of what fraction the use pays. A monopoly charter exists when, for example, a private or public hospital is protected from the entry of other hospitals into the community. The customer must have choice.

14

WORKERS IN THE NOT-FOR-PROFIT FIRM

There is a characteristic of economic life in the profit-seeking sector that controls what one receives in payment for services rendered. That is, over the long run an institution will not be willing to pay any individual (or, in the case of collective bargaining, any one factor of production) more than what that particular factor adds to revenue as a direct result of his or her efforts. In other words, if you work behind the counter at Burger King, the net revenue that you are responsible for generating in the company must be greater than or equal to your salary. In the long run, if this is not the case, you will find yourself not working at Burger King. Your value to the organization must at least be equal to what you are paid. You could lose your job, however, in spite of your efforts if the public became disenchanted with the Whopper.

In general, not-for-profit firms are also subject to the above mentioned characteristic of economic life. But the not-for-profit firm derives some part of its budget other than from the direct sale of its services to customers. Consequently, suppliers of resources to the not-for-profit firm have an opportunity to affect the payment to themselves by influencing the individuals who grant the budget to the organization. The purpose of this chapter is to analyze this influence through "political" activity in general and through collective bargaining in particular.

A not-for-profit firm must be funded. Unfortunately, pleasing the user of the service is not always the most direct way for employees to ensure promotion, raises and job security. In many instances, it might be a complete waste of time. In addition, the question "Who is the customer?" is never really clear. Is it the welfare client or the community? Is it the student or the parents of the students? Is it the patient in a hospital or the doctors who send their patients there? One thing, however, is certain. If a substantial part of the budget is determined by a sponsor, such as the legislature or board, then effort must be expended in pleasing them. In addition, the most effective and efficient program in the state or community, dearly appreciated by all its users, may not survive a budget cut or change in priorities on the part of the sponsoring organization. Under the circumstances, it is not surprising to find that employees in not-for-profit organizations are heavily involved in political activity.

Public employees are limited in the extent to which they may become personally involved in politics. Federal employees are technically prohibited by the Hatch Act, passed in 1939, from engaging in political campaigns. In 1940, Congress extended this restriction to state and local government employees whose salaries are paid from federal funds. Many states and cities have also enacted "little Hatch acts." These laws, intended to protect government employees from being forced to contribute to political campaigns or to work on behalf of politicians, have also been interpreted as prohibiting government employees from running for public office.

It is believed by some that the Hatch Act needlessly restricts the freedom of public employees, yet other individuals question whether or not civil servants should even be permitted to vote, much less engage in political activity. These individuals question the conflict of interest civil servants have in expansion. It is unlikely, however, that the civil service will be disenfranchised!

The "political" influence of resource suppliers in the private not-for-profit firm is equally significant. For example, should the president of the local firm that sells business forms to an institution be a member of its board of trustees? Should a faculty member sit on the board of an educational institution? "Why not?" you might answer, "These individuals certainly are concerned about the survival of the organization and have more interest than someone from out-of-town with a briefcase who visits two or three times a year." However, the effectiveness of the organization, whether it is involved in health care, education, credit, etc., is really a separate issue from the personal interests of those who work for the organization or supply it with services. Happy workers do not guarantee the delivery of the intended product or service.

But who owns the not-for-profit firm? The public not-for-profit firm is clearly owned by the taxpayer. But the monitoring role assigned to elected officials is difficult. The private not-for-profit firm may be owned by a religious community or the members of an organization. Some of these firms are monitored and others are not. Not-for-profit firms, which are not closely monitored, generally fail if they have to depend on customer fees. Many educational institutions which divorced themselves from their church affiliations have not survived. Heavily endowed organizations or ones that can tax their members, however, can survive indefinitely as worker run cooperatives. One may make the case that Harvard, the Rockefeller Foundation, the Teamster's Union, and government agencies are good examples.

Collective Bargaining

Since 1965 a rapid and dramatic rise in the unionization of government employees has occurred at Federal, state, and local levels. In less than a decade of intensive organizational activity, unions and associations in the public sector have succeeded in organizing a higher proportion of employees than have been organized in the private sector in thirty-five years of protection and encouragement under the National Labor Relations Act. About one-fourth of all private wage and salary workers belong to labor unions. By comparison, one-half of all federal employees are union members, and an even higher proportion of the nation's school teachers belong to either the National Education Association or the American Federation of Teachers. The fact that the public sector has been providing an expanding number of jobs relative to total employment has undoubtedly contributed to this rise in unionization. However, there are special aspects to the not-for-profit firm that are conducive to such organization.

What exactly have been the effects on wages and jobs in the private sector due to unions? Some maintain that the observed increases in wages through the twentieth century, as well as the percentage increase of wages as part of gross national product, would have occurred in the absence of unions. The rise would have been generated by increases in labor productivity due to technology. Higher wages are also a reflection of capital that is relatively abundant and labor that is relatively scarce.

Not all workers who organize and, therefore, have their contracts negotiated collectively stand to gain. In fact, if there is no change in the total amount of benefits allocated to labor in a particular organization, then, to the extent that salaries become more uniform, those who would have received higher than average salaries will be hurt by organization. In the public sector, however, any doubts about the minor benefits or losses in wages and salaries from a general or individual viewpoint are swamped by the enormous gains to be made by political activity in the public not-for-profit firm.

All state councils of the American Federation of State, County and Municipal Employees (AFSCME) engage in political activities as does the union's central Committee on Political Education. These political activities include the endorsement of candidates, distribution of voting records, contributions of manpower and occasionally funds in election campaigns, and invitations to candidates to address union meetings. All of the councils engage in some form of lobbying and testify before legislative committees and similar bodies.

Employee associations are of more significance than unions in the not-for-profit sector. The term employee association refers to some state organizations but includes organizations such as the American Nurses Association, the National Education Association, and the American Association of University Professors. Employee associations, unlike unions, are presumably not active politically. They rarely endorse candidates for elective office, contribute funds to political campaigns, provide manpower to help get out the vote, mail campaign literature, or perform the many other tasks that are important in elections. However, they do engage in lobbying in the legislatures, present testimony at legislative hearings and committee meetings, and try to influence votes on specific bills that affect their members.

Professional associations use a form of rhetoric that appears to be above political interest and divorced from issues outside their areas of competency. However, pushing for the health needs of the nation and increasing the per capita contribution to higher education are really just lunchbox issues on the part of some associations. And evidently, such political activity yields benefits for their numbers. (But unions and employee associations are themselves not-for-profit and thus the subject of this book!)

It is important to recognize the political activity of associations of employees of not-for-profit firms as an attempt to increase or maintain the demand for their services. These activities are aimed at the sponsors of the organization responsible for funding. However, one must not be so cynical as to assume that the purpose of the organizations are purely "political." They are concerned with negotiating a work contract between employees and the not-for-profit firm. In addition, employee associations set standards for their profession.

Employees of not-for-profit organizations are often in an extremely vulnerable position with respect to negotiating their contract. It is often the case, particularly in government employment, that they are hired monopsonistically. This means that there is only one buyer of their services and hence they must accept the contract offered or get out of that line of work. Of course, the solution to this monopsonistic position would be the proliferation of all types of not-for-profit firms both public and private. Surprisingly, employees of public institutions see private institutions as threats rather than potential employment opportunities. This strong opposition to private institutions by public employees leads one to believe that the monopsonistic power of the government is not being exercised with respect to wages adjusted for the degree of job security.

Permit us to discuss the mundane business of salary determination. As it appears in the comic strips, you usually go to the boss, manager, or administrator and work out what you will be paid. The agreement is usually between you and the boss and generally it is not considered appropriate to discuss salary with coworkers. From the viewpoint of the individual worker, this secrecy keeps him or her in blissful ignorance of those making more. Or, it permits one to avoid the jealousy of coworkers who covet the $36 net a year extra you are getting. The administration can either prefer the option of using the now proverbial $36 to retain superstars on the staff, encourage the diligent, or attract a hot shot from the outside. On the other hand, the administration could view the whole process of negotiating contracts each year as a waste of their time and prefer to deal with the designated bargaining agent of the staff. This is what is know as *collective bargaining*.

Collective bargaining agreements assume a variety of forms. Some agreements are amazingly brief, covering two or three typewritten pages; others are highly detailed, involving only a local union or a single plant; others set wages, hours, and working conditions for entire industries. There is no such thing as a typical collective bargaining agreement. Nevertheless, each agreement generally includes several articles, similar to those presented in Illustration 14-1. These articles are representative of those topics included in all collective bargaining agreements by and between the administration and the bargaining unit of professional employees.

Most comprehensive state laws governing collective bargaining in public employment follow the National Labor Relations Act in their procedures for designating which bargaining agent of the employees they will negotiate with. Either the organization can demonstrate that its members include more than one-half of the members of the agency or, if necessary, a secret ballot is conducted to determine which bargaining agent will represent the employees.

In many not-for-profit firms, the employees will vote first to decide if they favor collective bargaining and then again to determine the bargaining agent. In some states, such as Pennsylvania, all state agencies must negotiate contracts collectively. This attitude of government employers toward organization is undoubtedly a major factor in the success of employee organizations in public sector elections. There have been a relatively small number of charges of unfair labor practices by unions against public employers.

Illustration 14-1

Articles Included in a Collective Bargaining Contract Between a Not-For-Profit Firm and its Professional Employees

Article I: *Definitions.* The terms administration, staff, bargaining unit, and part-time staff are explained.

Article II: *Recognition of Unit.* In this, or in several following articles, the administration agrees to recognize the bargaining unit, provide it with necessary information, and permit the unit to use some of the firm's facilities.

Article III: *Guarantee of Rights.* Provides for the preagreement rights of the professional staff and no discrimination against any member or any applicant.

Article IV: *Grievance and Arbitration.* Defining a grievance as a dispute concerning the interpretation, application or alleged violation of the agreement, the formal grievance procedure is outlined and a permanent arbitrator may be named.

Article V: *No Strikes—No Lockouts.*

Article VI: *Compensation.* A complete salary schedule for all staff covered in the contract is presented. Following articles may outline the schedule of payments and allow for increased base salaries for certain staff members.

Article VII: *Fringe Benefits.*

Article VIII: *Professional Staff Information, Facilities, and Privileges.*

Article IX: *Workload.*

Article X: *Minimum Terms.* A statement to the effect that the administration will not employ a member on terms less favorable than those specified in the agreement.

Article XI: *Interest Succession.* Outlines the responsibility of newly appointed parties to follow the terms of the agreement.

Article XII: *Separability.* If, for some reason, one part of the agreement is not in effect, the remaining parts continue to be binding.

Article XIII: *Ratification.*

Article XIV: *Effective Date and Duration.*

15

CHECK PLEASE? THE BUDGET REVIEW

PROCESS

There is no bottom line (a statement of profit or loss) in a not-for-profit firm. Hence, accounting practices in the not-for-profit firm focus on judging whether resources have been used in desirable or prescribed ways, rather than on evaluating the results of their use. Evaluating the effectiveness of the organization is difficult so the sponsoring organization either passively approves the budget the administration prepares or, on the other hand, demands item-by-item control (down to the last paper clip) in the acquisition and disposal of resources. In this chapter the mechanics of budget preparation in not-for-profit firms are outlined followed by some comments on the relationship of a firm to its sponsor and on accounting practices.

Preparing the Budget

In this book, we have defined an administrator as one who is responsible for preparing and overseeing a separate identifiable budget. A new administrator is often offered unsolicited advice, somewhat facetiously, in the form of two cardinal rules. First, in preparing a budget proposal, take this year's budget and mark up each item by some multiple. Secondly, under no circumstances leave any item in the current budget unspent.

The naive administrator who holds the line on spending in his department is surprised when his supervisors in the agency are annoyed and exasperated with his parsimoniousness. Unfortunately, an administrator often has no clear way of demonstrating that the department which did not exhaust its budget maintained the same quantity and quality of service as one that spent everything. Furthermore, even if the level of service was maintained, the particular agency of which the department is a part may forfeit the unspent funds. Worse still, their total appropriation may be reduced the following year. In fact, the person in the agency who comes up with more creative projects on which to spend money is frequently rewarded.

Is there hope for efforts to constrain costs coming from within the not-for-profit firm? Generally, no. The not-for-profit firm does not operate in a market but rather in a political environment. The best strategy from the point of view of the firm is not to reveal cost, to overestimate demand, and to allow the sponsoring organization to determine how far it is willing to go in subsidizing the agency. Cost minimizing can, however, be forced from the outside on the not-for-profit firm by reduced appropriations and market-type competition among agencies.

A budget is a document which looks into the future. It can be a means by which not-for-profit firms are guided so as to produce intended consequences. This type of control necessitates the preparation of a detailed plan of operations. For example, the budget process of a not-for-profit firm begins with item-by-item estimates of the amounts of expenditures required for the production of the service. The proposed budget is then reviewed by the sponsor to approve, modify, or reject it. When the budget has been approved, the amounts appropriated are the limits of expenditures that may be incurred for each item in the budget.

Budgets basically are of two types: *line item* or *lump sum*. Line item budgeting requires listing every single position and piece of equipment on a separate line in the expenditure estimates. The sponsor reviewing the budget strikes out or approves individual items. The administrator charged with overseeing the budget may not transfer funds between items nor, in some cases, from one category of expense to another. In a school district, for example, budget approvals for staff may be switched at administrative discretion between janitors and clerks but not from salaries to school supplies. Line item budgeting provides the sponsor with maximum control over expenditures within the agency. But the sponsor may not choose to use this control effectively or he or she may not know how to use it effectively.

With lump sum budgeting transfers of funds may be made not only between budget items but even between projects. In many firms, lump sum budgeting is used along with a budget format that uses a category or object of expenditure approach. The sponsor may take the option of restricting the amounts that can be spent for certain purposes. For example, the sponsor of an educational firm may approve a sum for the professional development of faculty but restrict the amount spent for overseas travel.

The typical budget of a not-for-profit firm first details positions to be filled and secondly recommends amounts to be spent on non-personnel items. Usually there are three columns: last year, the present year and the proposed year. Generally, a not-for-profit firm does not have to justify in the budget what they are trying to accomplish with the funds.

Note the sample budget presented in Table 15-1. Table 15-2 is the budget of a department within an institution. If the department is an auxiliary activity, like a bookstore in a university, it is important to know the extent to which these activities support themselves or how much they contribute to the general functioning of the firm.

Table 15-1. Sample Budget of a Not-For-Profit Firm: The Case of a Church

	Last Year			Present Year			Proposed Year		
	General	*Restricted Activities*	*Total*	*General*	*Restricted Activities*	*Total*	*General*	*Restricted Activities*	*Total*
Revenues									
Sunday school collections	XX	XX	XXX	XX	XX	XXX	XX	XX	XXX
Plate offerings	XX	XX	XXX	XX	XX	XXX	XX	XX	XXX
Pledges for 19__	XX	XX	XXX	XX	XX	XXX	XX	XX	XXX
Pledges for 19__	XX	XX	XXX	XX	XX	XXX	XX	XX	XXX
Miscellaneous	XX	XX	XXX	XX	XX	XXX	XX	XX	XXX
Total revenues	XX	XX	XXX	XX	XX	XXX	XX	XX	XXX
Expenditures									
Benevolences	XX	XX	XXX	XX	XX	XXX	XX	XX	XXX
Christian education									
Literature	XX	XX	XXX	XX	XX	XXX	XX	XX	XXX
Church school supplies	XX	XX	XXX	XX	XX	XXX	XX	XX	XXX
Conference and camp fund	XX	XX	XXX	XX	XX	XXX	XX	XX	XXX
Outside speakers and leaders	XX	XX	XXX	XX	XX	XXX	XX	XX	XXX
Parties and recreation	XX	XX	XXX	XX	XX	XXX	XX	XX	XXX
Miscellaneous	XX	XX	XXX	XX	XX	XXX	XX	XX	XXX
Total	XX	XX	XXX	XX	XX	XXX	XX	XX	XXX

Music	XX	XX	XX	XXX	XX	XX	XX	XXX
Staff								
Minister	XX	XX	XX	XXX	XX	XX	XX	XXX
Minister of education	XX	XX	XX	XXX	XX	XX	XX	XXX
Secretary	XX	XX	XX	XXX	XX	XX	XX	XXX
Janitor and maid	XX	XX	XX	XXX	XX	XX	XX	XXX
Total	XX	XX	XX	XXX	XX	XX	XX	XXX
Current expenses								
Printing and office supplies	XX	XX	XX	XXX	XX	XX	XX	XXX
Custodian supplies and services	XX	XX	XX	XXX	XX	XX	XX	XXX
Miscellaneous	XX	XX	XX	XXX	XX	XX	XX	XXX
Total	XX	XX	XX	XXX	XX	XX	XX	XXX
Building								
Insurance (real estate and auto)	XX	XX	XX	XXX	XX	XX	XX	XXX
Utilities	XX	XX	XX	XXX	XX	XX	XX	XXX
Maintenance	XX	XX	XX	XXX	XX	XX	XX	XXX
Total	XX	XX	XX	XXX	XX	XX	XX	XXX
Debt retirement	XX	XX	XX	XXX	XX	XX	XX	XXX
Total expenditures	XX	XX	XX	XXX	XX	XX	XX	XXX
Excess of revenues over expenditures	XX	XX	XX	XXX	XX	XX	XX	XXX

Table 15-2. Sample Auxiliary Service or Department Budget Within A
Not-For-Profit Firm

Revenues		
Endowment income		$XXXX
Contributions		XXXX
Fees for services		XXXX
Other sources		XXXX
Total revenue		XXXX
Sustentation expenditures		
Fund raising costs	$XXX	
Allocated administrative costs	XXX	
Revenue available for intended services		XXXX
		$XXXX
Expenditures for services		
Function one	$XXX	
Function two	XXX	
Etc.	XXX	
Unexpended or overexpended amount	XXX	$XXXX

Accounting Practices

The accounting objective in the not-for-profit firm stresses the matching of costs and revenues in order to account for the acquisition and disposal of resources. Consequently, most not-for-profit firms rely on statements showing revenue and expenses. However, there is a tendency for organizations that rely for a large part of their revenue on user fees, like hospitals, to use formulas to project income derived from the sales of their services.

Not-for profit firms in general are characterized by the use of fund-accounting techniques. These techniques separate the resources of the organization into separate self-balancing fund entities. Instead of being concerned with one general ledger, the accounts of not-for-profit firms will have a separate self-balancing group of ledger accounts for each fund entity. A fund is a sum of money or other resources segregated for the purpose of carrying on specific activities in accordance with special restrictions and constituting an independent fiscal and accounting unit. The building funds of churches are a good example. Many not-for-profit firms agree to contributor stipulations that require the use of separate accounting entities.

Even if a separate fund is not set up, a not-for-profit firm permits a contributor or sponsor to designate specific claims against some assets. Note the inclusion of a column for restricted funds in Table 15-1. Some revenue sources like Sunday school collections and miscellaneous donations are reserved for special uses. Similarly, a decision may be made such that the proceeds from football bowl games in a university be earmarked for minority scholarships. Then an internal-restriction account is set up that indicates a requirement to use either assets or specified amounts of total assets in a certain manner.

Not-for-profit firms generally do not record depreciation. Capital expenditures are charged off in the period when they are incurred or paid. Similarly, only readily appropriable assets and outstanding obligations are shown in their reports rather than all accrued and prepaid items.

Not-for-profit firms typically carry on a number of activities not directly related to their primary function. Dormitories, intercollegiate athletics and bookstores are examples of such auxiliary activities in colleges and universities. It is important to know the extent to which these auxiliary activities subsidize or are subsidized by the educational function of the institution. Separate accounts or funds are maintained for these activities. Sometimes, even at government institutions, these accounts are closed to the public.

Besides auxiliary activities, a more complex problem is associated with a not-for-profit firm pursuing several goals. Research and teaching in a university is financed by a combination of outside grants, tax funds and student fees. Even the best accounting practices operate on assumptions that estimate overhead. Hence, it is difficult to isolate whether one activity is subsidizing another or vice versa.

Budgets and Sponsors

For weeks before Board meetings in many not-for-profit firms, and perhaps in profit-seeking ones as well, the administrators direct almost all their energies towards getting ready to dazzle the visitors. Chief administrators are hired by the Board. However, the role of the board varies significantly from firm to firm, because in not-for-profit firms the ownership of the institution is not clear.

The board is particularly important in those not-for-profit firms that derive a large fraction of their total budget from a sponsoring organization that the board truly represents. School boards are the best example. The board not only approves allocation of items in the budget but the size of the budget. Furthermore, the board can coerce the residents to pay for the schools through taxes. The potential for control by some not-for-profit boards far exceed that of the boards of a corporation which represents only the owners. In the profit-seeking sector customers are generally free to buy or not buy the product.

Approximately two thirds of the funding for many not-for-profit agencies is the State Legislature, the United Fund, or Washington. Hence, the role of the board is often reduced to rubber stamping administrators' policy recommendations.

In some cases, as when a not-for-profit firm has been founded by a religious organization, that organization will retain certain rights. In other words, there may exist a two-tiered board. For example, the supra-board representing the interests of the founders may retain a veto over the choice of the Board for president.

Where do board officers, charged with critical review of not-for-profit firms, come from? They may be appointed by the chief administrator himself or appointed by the duly elected head of the wider constituency sponsoring the agency. Members of a board of commissioners for municipal parks, for example, may be appointed by the park supervisor himself or the mayor.

The larger constituency may elect some board members directly. Two members of a school board or the board of trustees may be elected by the citizens or the alumni respectively. Users of the agency may also be represented and, less frequently, professionals who work for the firm.

PART V

WHAT TO DO . . .
WHAT TO DO

16

INFORMATION SYSTEMS I

Managerial planning techniques, called by many different names, have developed and spread rapidly around the world during the last fifteen or twenty years, both among profit-seeking and not-for-profit organizations. This chapter and Chapter 17 will explain planning from the viewpoint of a not-for-profit firm and summarize those planning techniques used by many of them. Every individual and every organization, both profit-seeking and not-for-profit, plans. The decisions made by administrators presuppose some future environment of the organization and are thus crude plans in themselves.

Planning is only a means to help administrators make decisions. It is not a robot-like substitute for administrators to blindly use in selecting among alternative courses of action. Planning in the not-for-profit sector is different from a profit-seeking producer's planning, because in not-for-profit firms, planning is usually a group process; it involves administrators, sponsoring agencies, pressure groups and employees. The planning process includes choosing problems for solution, deciding on the alternative solutions, and developing incentives to ensure the implementation of the solutions.

The selection of goals, the first step in any planning system, is relatively easy in the profit-seeking firm. The corporation seeks to maximize the net benefit of its stockholders in some long term sense. In the not-for-profit firm, however, the nature of goals is quite different. These goals are often complex, rapidly changing, difficult to measure, and multi-faceted. Regardless of how difficult goal setting is to a not-for-profit firm, goals are of primary importance in managing the firm.

Goals could be described as the desired ends or the results towards which some behavior is directed. Note that the mere presence of goals in a not-for-profit organization does not guarantee any role for them in improving administrative effectiveness or efficiency. All of us are familiar with situations where goals are loudly and enthusiastically proclaimed, only to be quickly ignored or altogether forgotten. The benefits of goals in a planning system come from their influence on the behavior of administrators. Goals that indicate to managers what they should be doing serve as targets for behavior, and to the extent they do serve as real targets for behavior, job behavior can become purposeful and productive. In order for goals to influence administrators, two conditions must be met. First, the administrators must consider or be forced to consider the attainment important. Secondly, the administrators must believe that the level of his effort has some relationship to actually achieving the goals.

Goals, defined in terms of output measures in not-for-profit firms, can serve as the standard against which to evaluate administrative performance. A not-for-profit firm which has no goals has effectively eliminated administrative accountability. Administrators of these firms might quite reasonably be reluctant to state goals explicity; first, because it is difficult to do so, and, secondly, because goals hold the administration to a standard of performance.

One of the difficulties encountered in not-for-profit firm planning is to distinguish between goals and the means towards those goals. Medical doctors (means) are not the same as healthier individuals (goals). The job of the not-for-profit administrator is first to convert vague desires into goals and secondly to convert inputs (means) into predictable outputs.

Consider the administrator faced with "reducing the crime rate" given a fixed budget. The task is to convert the desire for a lower crime rate into a ranked and weighted set of goals or ends. Given these goals, the administrator would choose among various combinations of inputs (policemen, patrol cars, special courses for police, etc.) that combination minimizing the crime rate. One must realize that the goal (reducing the crime rate) and the inputs (means) are often both variables. The difficulty for the administrator is not often merely one of choosing the "optimal" set of inputs (means), but rather of obtaining an agreement from the group involved in decision making, on a set of goals and desires, and the various outcomes of different sets of inputs.

The not-for-profit administrator who wishes to make good decisions will ultimately follow these five planning rules:

1. Specify the goals desired.
2. Quantify the goals or select targets and indicators as suggested in Chapter 18.
3. Specify and quantify the means for achieving the desired goals.
4. Specify constraints, ethical and environmental, likely to affect planning.
5. Consider the spillover or side effect of the plan.

Consider the case of the Horsham Methodist Church in Horsham, England. Although it is unusual for a church to plan in the formal sense, this small (250 member) church engaged in a formal planning system in early 1972. The members of the community felt that a plan would help the church in two ways. First, they wanted to examine their role in Horsham to see whether they were doing what they felt was an appropriate job and, secondly, they wished to use planning as a tool to help them more effectively achieve their goals. A planning system was set up for the church which followed the five rules outlined above. Three groups were involved in the planning process: first, a Planning Committee, made up of about ten members of the community; secondly, a leader's meeting, which was a group of about ten members of the community elected to act as the ruling authority for the church; finally, the church members themselves. The Planning Committee performed those tasks outlined in Table 16-1. The Planning Committee defined the objectives of the church and selected proxies as substitutes for goals that could not be quantified.

The authors recall a church in Blacksburg, Virginia, which had a set of proxies placed on a board outside its place of worship, and updated each Sunday. Included as proxies on the board were the numbers of members of the congregation present on Sunday as compared with the number of members present on that Sunday one year previously. Also included was the number of members of the congregation attending which brought Bibles to the meeting, the dollar size of the collection the previous Sunday, and the number of children attending Sunday School. Undoubtedly it would be difficult to post a quantification of the real objective of the church, such as "the number of souls saved." Evidently, the items listed on the board were deemed by the congregation and the minister to be the best proxies available for the ultimate goal.

Notice also, in the case of the Horsham planning program, that the church identified activities in relation to the objectives. That is, it specified those activities which it felt directly contributed to the objectives of the church, thereby quantifying the means for achieving the goals of the church. In addition, the church also performed an environmental analysis which took the form of studying population trends, the development of Horsham, the areas where new housing estates might be built, and the way in which old people and youth were being cared for. The environmental condition suggested to the church that there was a need in the community for scouting facilities and that the distance to church inconvenienced members living in the new developments. Demographic analysis also suggested that

Sunday School attendance could increase rather rapidly in coming years. Finally, the Horsham plan also included a provision for monitoring the progress towards the goals of the planning program. Included in this concept of monitoring the progress was the consideration of the effect that the plan was having on institutions other than the Horsham church.

The remainder of this chapter will be a survey of those planning tools which have commonly been used by not-for-profit firms in recent years. The techniques discussed will be planning, programming and budgeting systems (PPBS), zero-based budgeting (ZBB), and operations research.

Table 16-1   Planning Programme (Horsham Methodist Church)

Planning Committee	*Leaders' Meeting*	*Church Members*
1. Define Task		
2. Define Objectives		
	3. Provisional Approval of Objectives	
4. Study Facts About Church		
5. Environmental Analysis		
6. Identify Current Activities in Relation to Objectives		
	7. Progress Report to Leaders' Meeting	
8. Programme for Church Meeting		
		9. Adopt Objectives
		10. Assess Strengths and Weaknesses
		11. Identify Projects
	14. Recommendations Approved	
		15. Implement

Source: "Corporate Planning For A Church," David E. Hussey, *Long Range Planning* (April, 1974), 61-64.

Planning, Programming, Budgeting Systems

PPBS had its beginning in the Department of Defense of the United States Government, under Secretary Robert McNamara. It is a system for assisting administrators to choose among alternative programs related to the use of resources. It does not actually make the choices. Numerous other Federal Government agencies and not-for-profit institutions have adopted PPBS as part of their planning system. We may think of a PPBS system as comprised of five separate steps.

As a first step, PPBS calls for a specification of the objectives of the institution. These should be so stated so that they are really ends desired by the institution. For instance, the National Highway Traffic Safety Administration (NHTSA) is charged by the Federal Government with automobile safety in the United States. It might be inclined to list, as one of its objectives, the installation of seat belts in each and every car produced in the United States. Actually, the installation of seat belts is a means of obtaining the objective of automobile safety. An institution must be clear in specifying objectives under a PPBS system, so as not to confuse means (such as the installation of seat belts) with ends (such as automobile safety). Once an objective, such as automobile safety, is accepted, it becomes possible to analyze seat belts, improved highways, additional driver training, more stringent law enforcement and so on, as components of an effective program of automobile safety.

The second step in a PPBS system is to analyze the actual output of the institution in terms of the stated objectives. The emphasis here is on examining the output's relationship with the ultimate objectives. In what specific way, for instance, is automobile safety promoted by the installation of seat belts? How many accidents are prevented? How many accidents result in less injury? How many lives are actually saved?

Measuring the cost of a particular program is the third step in a PPBS system. In the case of automobile safety, certainly the budget of the NHTSA would be part of the direct cost to Americans of automobile safety. Indirect costs also, however, are important to consider in any PPBS system. The increased prices charged by automobile companies as a result of regulations requiring seat belts to be installed must also be included as a cost of automobile safety in a PPBS system.

The most important step in a PPBS system is the fourth step, and that is to analyze alternatives, searching for those which have the greatest effectiveness in achieving the basic objectives. In the automobile safety case, for example, the NHTSA should be comparing the effectiveness of automobile seat belts with improvements in highways or advances in the training of auto-mobile drivers. There is no mandate that only one of the alternatives should be chosen, but there is an emphasis on choosing those alternatives which are most effective. It is the competition among alternatives which is crucial to the success of a PPBS system.

The final element in a PPBS system is to establish the process outlined above in a systematic way so that it occurs repetitiously over time. Program structures can be designed for any organi-zation, including not-for-profit hospitals, schools, universities and foundations.

As an example of PPBS's use in the not-for-profit sector, consider the use of program budgeting in higher education. Program budgeting focuses on the outcome of products of higher education and their unit costs.[1] The chief products of universities in the United States are the degrees awarded in different majors. PPBS may be used to determine the per degree cost for each major in which degrees are awarded. As part of this cost analysis, it would be necessary to examine what courses are commonly chosen by students majoring in each discipline, what the enrollments in these courses are, what the per course salaries of the faculty members who teach the courses are, and what

[1]This use of PPBS in higher education is detailed in ''New Tools and Techniques in University Administration,'' *Educational Record*, Winter 1974.

fraction of general institutional expenditures (overhead) is attributable to majors in that area. With information available about the costs of existing majors, PPBS draws attention to the appropriate "mix" of various program elements that are cost related. These elements would include the diversity of offerings, the size of class sections, faculty work load, the balance of instructional methods, the number of required courses, salary schedules, and the levels of support activities. These elements of the "mix" are essentially the means to the end of producing educated graduates.

Under PPBS, the direct costs of a particular major are arrived at by determining the cost of the credit hours produced by the various departments for each major. Indirect costs are also included in the total cost for each major. PPBS leads to a focus on the quality of the output of programs in relation to their costs.

Table 16-2   Examples of Objectives Stated Quantitatively

Program Size Indicators:
—Classes or students taught by a faculty member
—Projects undertaken by a manager
—Full-time equivalent students attending a university
—Number of loans made by a credit union

Work Load Indicators:
—Number of judgments rendered by a court
—Number of automobile inspections performed
—Number of eye examinations given
—Number of hours a teacher spends in the classroom

Output Measures:
—Number of graduates from a university
—Number of lives saved by a safety program

Input Measures:
—Number of classrooms occupied
—Number of doses of vaccine administered
—Number of police cars on patrol

Performance Measures:
—Average time required for an ambulance to arrive
—Number of publications for a university professor
—Tons of garbage hauled

Perhaps one of the most difficult parts of a PPBS system to implement is that of stating the objectives in a quantifiable manner or assigning proxies for those outputs which can be measured. Table 16-2 is a list of examples which may prove useful.[2]

Zero Base Budgeting (ZBB)

Zero base budgeting is a planning process which requires each administrator to justify budget requests in detail, from scratch (zero base), and shifts the burden of proof to the administrator to justify why an expenditure should be made at all. The system, initiated by Peter Phyrr at Texas Instruments, Inc., requires that: (1) each activity be identified in a decision package (or program) that relates input with output; (2) each activity be evaluated by systematic analysis; and (3) all programs be ranked in order of performance. Zero base budgeting is a planning tool which requires bottom-to-top planning by the administrator of a not-for-profit firm.

Each fiscal year, before funds are actually allocated, every administrator begins with the assumption that all resources need to be justified. The process is accomplished formally by developing decision units, decision packages, and then by ranking the packages. A decision unit is a significant program, or it could be an individual department or, perhaps, the level of an organization. A decision package is combined with other decision packages to make up the total budget request for a particular decision unit. Each administrator uses these decision packages to review, evaluate and justify each and every pro-

---

[2]This list of program measures is found in *Systematic Analysis* by Graeme Taylor and Harley Hinrichs, Goodyear Publishing Company, 1972, pp. 151-152. This book also includes numerous other tips for implementing a PPBS program.

gram, project or activity. As part of the process of zero base budgeting, each administrator is required to examine alternative ways of performing the various activities and examining various levels of resource allocation which could be used in the decision packages.

The final step in the zero base budgeting process is that of ranking. Each administrator, after making up decision packages as outlined above, ranks each decision package which is included in the budget request. Decision packages are ranked and consolidated at each higher level of management. The final budget for the firm is made up of a list of packages in priority order. Each decision unit manager, during the fiscal year, checks the achievement toward the specified performance objectives of each decision package. Thus, zero base budgeting is a cost control system in addition to a planning system.

While zero base budgeting has been used by the United States Department of Agriculture since 1971, it has become exceedingly popular with all levels of city, state and federal government. This is largely because of its use by Jimmy Carter in Georgia in 1972 and its subsequent use, because of Carter's initiative, in the federal government since 1976.

Operations Research

Operations research, as it is called in the United States, or "operational research" in Great Britain (and often called "management science" in many universities) is the systematic application of quantitative methods, techniques and tools to the analysis of problems involving the operation of a management system. The objective of operations research in a not-for-profit firm would be to improve the effectiveness of the administrative system as a whole. However, it is used most often to plan and optimize a sub-set of the goals or objectives of an agency or organization. Operations research began in the 1940's, and its name reflects its first applications: the analysis and research of military operations.

Although no two managerial problems are identical, operations research has been successfully applied in many corporations and over a wide range of not-for-profit institutions. Many administrators indicate that their problems are unique. Underlying every application of operations research is the construction or the development of a *model*. A model may be thought of as a replica of an object. It may be an exact replica, or a stylized representation of the original object. Iconic models are those which look similar to the object being modeled. A model airplane which is a representation of the real, full-scale airplane could be thought of as an iconic model. While iconic models are sometimes used by operations researchers, it is more often the case that analog models, which are those models in which only some of the properties of the real object are retained, are more useful. A hand-held calculator which selects a random integer between one and six could be thought of as an analog model of a die (one of two dice).

A mathematical model is the type of analog model most often used in operations research. In a mathematical model, symbols or numbers may be used to represent certain characteristics of an original object or system. The purpose of a mathematical model in operations research is to help a manager understand and evaluate various alternatives efficiently.

The use of models in planning and decision making for not-for-profit administrators is especially important. The quantity of facts and figures the administrator is required to take into account and the difficulty of the decisions he is expected to make are enormous. The use of models allows the not-for-profit administrator to concentrate on the particular problem and the particular relationships involved in making a given decision.

A model allows the administrator to strip away all of the non-essential facts in a situation. Planning models should not be alien to most managers, because all of us resort to the use of models each day. A simple road map is a model which abstracts from the topographical reality of nature and presents the essentials which most motorists need to find their way, such as route numbers, distances and the locations of major cities. This road map can take the form of a plan, if an individual wishes to go from one point to another. The road map provides a technique in the form of a model for planning rational decisions.

The models used in operations research by not-for-profit administrators for planning and decision making are actually not much more difficult to use than the simple road map. Formal models allow the manager to concentrate on the most important variables in a situation and allow the manager to temporarily ignore the unimportant, but still present variables. The techniques we will examine in operations research, that is the models which we will examine, are those most often used by decision makers in the not-for-profit firm.[3] The techniques to be explained in Chapter 17 are linear programming, program evaluation and review technique (PERT), probability theory, or decision theory, and simulation.

---

[3]See "A Survey of Industrial OR/MS Activities in the 70's," reported by Thomas M. Cook and Robert A. Russell in the *Proceedings of the 8th Annual Conference of the American Institute for Decision Sciences*, Nov., 1976, pp. 122-124. See also the results reported by F. C. Weston in "*O.R. Techniques Relevent to Corporate Planning Function Practices, An Investigative Look,*" presented at 39th National Meeting, Operations Research Society of America, *Operations Research Bulletin*, Vol. 19, Suppl. 2, Spring 1971.

17

INFORMATION SYSTEMS II

Linear Programming

Every not-for-profit firm has to make decisions about how to allocate its resources. The not-for-profit firm which operates on a permanent basis with unlimited resources does not exist. Therefore, not-for-profit administrators must continuously allocate scarce resources to achieve their organization's goals. Linear Programming is a mathematical model for finding the best uses of an organization's resources. It is probably one of the most used techniques of operations research because there are many commercially available solution packages. A solution package is a programmed computer routine for which the user merely key-punches in the values of the variables. These commercially available linear programming packages will always find a solution, if one exists. If no solution exists, and that is a possibility, most of these packages will indicate to the administrator that the model is inconsistent.

There are three essential elements of a linear programming model:

1. Variables - Every linear programming problem has variables which the administrator is seeking to control. The variables are usually denoted by letters of the alphabet, with some subscripts. The variables traditionally answer such

questions as, how many nurses should be available in a hospital ward at various times during the day, or, how many firemen should be available at each of a number of fire stations in a city.

2. The objective function - This is a mathematical statement of the goals or objectives of the administrator. In linear programming situations, the objective function is either minimized or maximized. An example of an objective function would be to minimize the number of nurses reporting to a hospital ward during each reporting period, or to minimize the number of firemen in a given city consistent with a given level of service. Only a single objective or goal is considered in the objective function. There is only one objective function and, so, linear programming models reduce real world situations to single-purpose decision scenarios.

3. Constraints - These are mathematical statements that indicate the limitations placed on the manager or conditions which must be met in minimizing or maximizing the objective function. Examples of constraints would be the number of nurses needed in a hospital ward between midnight and 4:00 A.M., or, the minimum number of firemen required to staff a given fire station within a city at all times.

This type of programming is called *linear* because the objective function and the constraints in any program must be linear. This means that the contribution of each variable in the objective function and of each variable in the constraints is proportional to the value of the variable. For example, it must be assumed in the hospital ward situation that follows that two nurses may accomplish exactly double what a single nurse could do. In a fire station situation, it is assumed that two firemen can accomplish exactly double what a single fireman could. While this assumption of linearity is obviously not a replication of the real world, in most cases it is a close enough representation.

To illustrate a linear programming model, consider the following situation, outlined in Table 17-1. A hospital operates on a 24-hour basis. Based on estimates of the need for nurses throughout the 24-hour period, the administrator of a hospital feels that he requires a minimum number of employees during the given time periods.

Table 17-1   Linear Programming in Scheduling Nurses

Minimum Number of Nurses Required:

Time Period	Number Required
0:01 - 4:00	3
4:01 - 8:00	5
8:01 - 12:00	13
12:01 - 16:00	8
16:01 - 20:00	19
20:01 - 24:00	10

Total Number of Nurses Reporting During 24-Hour Period (objective):

$$Z = A + B + C + D + E + F$$

Z = the total overall number of nurses required by the hospital

A = the number of nurses reporting at 12:00 midnight
B = the number of nurses reporting at   4:00 A.M.
C = the number of nurses reporting at   8:00 A.M.
D = the number of nurses reporting at 12:00 Noon
E = the number of nurses reporting at   4:00 P.M.
F = the number of nurses reporting at   8:00 P.M.

Constraints:
$A + B \geq 5$
$B + C \geq 13$
$C + D \geq 8$
$D + E \geq 19$
$E + F \geq 10$
$A + F \geq 3$
$A, B, C, D, E, F \geq 0$

The objective constraint is a mathematical representation of what the administrator would like to minimize or maximize. In this case, the manager of the hospital would like to minimize the total number of nurses required. Because each nurse may be assumed to work only one 8-hour shift within a 24-hour period, we can assume that the total number of nurses reporting during a 24-hour period is the number of nurses required by the hospital. (Do not worry, at this point, that although nurses report every four hours each one works for eight hours.) This could mathematically be stated in the following way: $Z = A + B + C + D + E + F$.

This mathematical statement, then, is the function that the administrator would like to minimize; that is, he would like to pick values for "A" through "F" such that the value of "Z" is minimized. If this equation were the entire statement of the problem, the administrator's task would be simple, and to minimize "Z", he would choose to have no nurses report at "A", no nurses report at "B", and so on. Summing up the total number of nurses reporting then, would be zero. Following this procedure would clearly minimize the function! This, however, is only the objective function and is not the complete statement of the problem. While the manager wishes to minimize this function, there are certain other constraints, or side conditions, which must be met.

The constraints, or side conditions, may also be written as mathematical statements, in this case inequalities. Referring to the table, we can see that between the hours of 4:00 A.M. and 8:00 A.M., five nurses are required to be on duty. Now recall that each nurse is required to work a complete 8-hour shift after reporting. Thus, the number of nurses that will be available on the floor from 4:00 A.M. to 8:00 A.M. will be the sum of the nurses which have reported at 12:00 midnight and the nurses which have reported at 4:00 A.M. The nurses which reported at 12:00 midnight will be completing the last four hours of their 8-hour shift while the nurses arriving at 4:00 A.M. will be completing the first four hours of their 8-hour shift. Our first constraint could then be written as: A + B ≥ 5. This indicates that the number of nurses arriving at "A", plus the number of nurses arriving at "B", must be greater than or equal to five. This will satisfy the condition that we require at least five nurses between the hours of 4:00 A.M. and 8:00 A.M. Note that there will be five other constraints, one for each of the time periods.

There is one final consideration which is required in all linear programming problems. It is oftentimes called the non-negativity constraint, and refers to the fact that each of the variables we have chosen, "A" through "F", must never take on a value less than zero. This may be written as: A, B, C, D, E, F ≥ 0. Common sense would tell us that this must be the case. If "A", for instance, were to take on a value less than zero, that is, a negative value, say, minus one, this would indicate that the appropriate number of nurses to report at 12:00 Midnight would be minus one. This, of course, is nonsense, assuming that a nurse could not be sent home after 4 hours, and so we disallow any values for the variables in linear programming which are less than zero.

Note that each of the constraints listed above for this linear programming problem is an inequality rather than an equation. This is the case in most not-for-profit firm applications of linear programming because many problems cannot be expressed in the form of neat and precise equations. Inequalities suggest a more advanced type of mathematical relationship. The six inequality constraints set the lower limits on the number of nurses required during each time period of operation for the twenty-four hour hospital day.

Once the problem is set up as a linear programming problem, the administrator may use any one of a number of algorithms or computer packages to arrive at an optimal solution (there may be more than one optimal solution). One optimal solution for the above problem assigns a value of three to "A", that is, three nurses would report at 12:00 Midnight, a value of thirteen to

"B", that is, thirteen nurses would report at 4:00 A.M., a value of zero to "C", that is, no nurses would report at 8:00 A.M., a value of nine to "D", that is, nine nurses would report at Noon, a value of ten to "E", that is, ten nurses would report at 4:00 P.M., and a value of zero to "F", that is, no nurses would report at 8:00 P.M. The total number of nurses in this situation which the hospital would have to retain would be thirty-five.

Recall that no single nurse is allowed to work more than one eight-hour shift, and so the sum of all nurses reporting in a twenty-four hour period is the total number of nurses that the hospital would be required to retain on any given day. While there *are* other solutions to this particular problem, there is no other solution which would allow the hospital to meet the requirements listed in the table above *and use a total of fewer than thirty-five nurses.* The linear programming model, then, has allowed the administrator in this situation to choose an allocation of resources (nurses) that will meet his requirements *at the least cost to the hospital.*

Many computer programs today, in addition to providing the simple solutions to linear programs, also provide data to the manager as part of what is called a "sensitivity analysis." A sensitivity analysis of a linear programming solution answers questions of the "what if" variety. "What if," in the hospital case, one more nurse were required between Noon and 4:00 P.M.? The computer's solution to the hospital case problem would indicate how sensitive the solution it produced was with respect to slightly different values of the constraints. The computer actually solves the linear programming problem for slightly different values of the constraint equations. Then it compares the answers in those situations with the answer which it produced as the optimal solution for the constraints which it was originally given. Sensitivity analysis in the hospital case would indicate whether only minor rescheduling of the nurses would be required, should demand conditions change, or whether complete rescheduling of the nursing staff would be necessary.

As a second example of linear programming for a not-for-profit institution, consider the situation of portfolio selection for the manager of a state credit union.[4]

The manager of a state credit union is given the responsibility of maximizing the return to the shareholders of the credit union of a $100,000 portfolio, but he is constrained by state and federal law and the guidelines given him by the Board of Directors of the credit union. The investments available for this particular credit union are listed in Table 17-2.

To most credit unions, the last two investments are perhaps the most important. Signature loans to members consist of those loans made to members of the credit union, for which no security is offered. Secured loans to members are usually loans for automobiles which are secured by the title to the new or used automobile purchased by the credit union member. Also given in the table are the guidelines which the manager must follow in investing the $100,000. The Board of Directors of the credit union has felt that secured loans must account for at least 40% of the portfolio in order to minimize the default risk to the credit union. The Board of Directors has also stipulated that federal bonds must account for 20% of the portfolio in order to ensure some liquidity for withdrawals. Stocks are limited to 20% of the portfolio because of their inherent riskiness, and no one investment type may exceed 45% of the value of the total portfolio, following the ancient dictum, "Don't put all your eggs in one basket."

---

[4]See Chapter 10 in *Quantitative Approaches to Management* by Richard Levin and Charles Kirkpatrick, McGraw-Hill, Inc., (1978), pp. 288-348. Numerous linear programming situations and their solutions are lucidly explained by Levin and Kirkpatrick.

Table 17-2. Linear Programming in a Credit Union

INVESTMENT	SYMBOL	RETURN
Indiana and Michigan Electric Company Bonds	A	9.1
Indiana and Michigan Electric Company Preferred	B	8.3
FNMA Bonds (Federal National Mortgage Association)	C	8.6
Deposits at League Credit Union	D	6.0
Secured Loans (usually auto) to members	E	10.0
Signature Loans to members	F	12.0

Stocks are limited to 20% of portfolio.
No one investment category may exceed 45% of portfolio.
Secured loans must account for 40% of portfolio.
Federal Bonds must account for 20% of portfolio.

Maximize: Total Return = .091A + .083B + .086C
+ .060D + .100E + .120F

Subject to: A + B + C + D + E + F =

	100,000
B≤	20,000
E≥	40,000
E≤	45,000
C≥	20,000
C≤	45,000
A≤	45,000
D≤	45,000
F≤	45,000

A, B, C, D, E, F, ≥ 0

The objective function and the constraints which are required to solve this credit union linear programming problems are listed in Table 17-2.

Note that in this problem the first constraint ensures that the entire $100,000 will be invested and thus the constraint is written as an "equal to." The second constraint ensures that no more than 20%, or $20,000 of the $100,000 portfolio, will be invested in stocks. Constraints three and four ensure that at least 40% but no more than 45% of the porfolio will be invested in secured loans to members. Constraints five and six ensure that at least 20% but no more than 45% of the portfolio will be invested in federal bonds. Constraints seven, eight and nine ensure that no more than 45% of the portfolio will be invested in the remaining investment categories, that is, corporate bonds, deposits at the League Credit Union, and signature loans to members. The final constraint is of course the non-negativity condition which ensures that no variable "A" through "F" may take on a negative value. Keep in mind that it would not make sense if the optimal answer were to suggest that a minus $2,000 were to be invested in FNMA bonds.

Note in this formulation of a linear programming problem that it is possible to have both inequalitites and equalities as constraints in a single problem. The first constraint above is an equality while the remaining eight constraints are inequalities of either the "greater than" or "less than" formulation. Most commercially available solution packages for linear programming will accept constraints written in this fashion. In this case the answer or the optimal solution to this linear programming problem is almost obvious. The credit union manager would maximize the return on his investment and meet each of the constraints if he were to invest $40,000 in signature loans which return 12%, $40,000 in secured loans which return 10%, and $20,000 in FNMA bonds which return 8.6%. Over the course of a year the total interest earnings that he would net would be

$10,520 ($4,000 from the signature loans, $4,800 from the secured loans, and $1,720 from the bonds). In this particular situation there is no other combination of investments which would yield $10,520 or more *and* meet all of the constraints listed above.

PERT (Program Evaluation and Review Technique)

Development projects in not-for-profit firms usually consist of a number of inter-related tasks, some of which can be executed simultaneously and some of which can only be started after other tasks have been completed. Each task or activity takes some time to complete, and managers are often interested in the earliest time that a project can be completed and the feasibility of various alternative ways of completing the project. Many planning problems and scheduling problems such as occur in construction projects or in the maintenance of large facilities, or in the introduction of new services, etc., require coordinated planning which involves a sequencing of activities over time. PERT (Program Evaluation and Review Technique) was developed in 1958 to assist Navy managers in development and production of the Polaris missile. PERT involves the consideration of the times which various activities take and the scheduling of those activities with the realization that all activities may not be completed concurrently.

PERT is used by not-for-profit administrators for determining feasible schedules for various projects which are made up of inter-related activities. PERT is uniquely suitable for planning and scheduling projects which will take place only once. The technique involves constructing arrow diagrams (a network) representing the individual activities required to proceed from the beginning of a project to its end. A PERT network shows all of the interdependencies that exist among the individual activities. In complicated situations computer programs are often utilized to assemble and sort out the information in a PERT study.

The network diagram is correctly called a model in the sense described above. It is a representation of an entire project emphasizing the times that each of the activities making up the project take and the unique relationships between the activities (i.e. some activities must preceed and others must follow certain activities). The PERT network is a geometric representation resembling a map of a project and may be read by the administrator for planning purposes. Critical activities deserve the most attention from the manager because these activities could delay the completion of the entire project.

PERT has been successfully used to model and plan traffic flows, to minimize congestion in cities, to determine the shortest pickup and delivery routes for sanitation trucks, and for the optimal routing of schoolbuses in large cities. The federal government is a major user of PERT by virtue of the fact that many government contracts stipulate payment to the major contractor on many projects concurrent with progress followed along a PERT network. PERT networks are also used to plan space vehicle construction, to help prepare contract bids, and to aid in the optimal routing of medical patients for examination and treatment.

An abbreviated case study will demonstrate the essentials of a PERT network.[5] Suppose that you are the government project manager for the construction of a new munitions plant. The construction of the entire plant may be referred to as a "project."

Table 17-3 lists the seven activities which must be completed before the project of building the munitions plant itself is

---

[5]For more detailed examples and explanations of PERT see Ulysses Knotts, JR. and Ernest Swift, *Management Science for Decisions*, Allyn and Bacon, 1978, Chapter 11.

complete. An "activity" in PERT language is any portion of a project which consumes time and resources and has some specific beginning point and a specific ending point. An activity is the work necessary to progress from one situation in time to another situation. The activity entitled "lay foundation" is a portion of the munitions plant project which, according to the table, is expected to take four days to complete. At the end of the four-day period it is expected that the foundation will have been laid. Graphically an activity is represented by an arrow with some description of the time estimate written alongside the arrow. For the activity "lay foundation" an arrow is drawn running from left to right on the lefthand side of the accompanying diagram, and the number 4 (the expected time to complete the activity) is placed beneath the arrow.

An "event" in PERT language signifies either the beginning or the completion of an activity or a number of activities, and it occurs at an instantaneous point in time. In themselves events take no time to complete and are normally represented by a numbered circle. The activity "lay foundation" is described by the events 1 and 2 and is referred to as activity 1,2. The 1 therefore signifies the beginning of the activity of laying the foundation, while 2 signifies its completion. Some events will represent the completion of more than one activity.

In Table 17-3, event number 4 represents the completion of two activities, activity 3,4 closing in the walls and activity 2,4 installing the floor. In order for event 4 to take place, both activity 3,4 and activity 2,4 must have taken place. An event is always represented by a single number such as (1). An activity is always represented by a pair of numbers such as (1,2).

The graphical representation of the entire project of building the munitions plant which shows the interrelationships of all the activities and their associated times is called a network and is represented in Table 17-3. The network may be appropriately read from left to right and indicates that event 1 is the beginning of the project; event 6 is the completion of the entire project. For the project to have been completed, each and every activity in the network must have been completed.

Table 17-3. Pert Network for a Munitions Plant

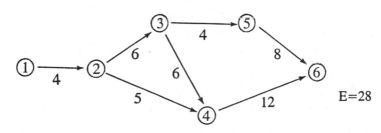

Activity Symbol	Activity	Expected Time to Complete
1,2	lay foundation	4 days
2,3	box walls	6 days
2,4	install floor	5 days
3,4	close in walls	6 days
3,5	roof	4 days
4,6	finish interior	12 days
5,6	finish exterior	8 days

Notice that the arrangement of the activities is dictated by the technology of the situation. Roofing the structure, activity 3,5 for instance, may not take place until after the foundation is laid (activity 1,2) and the walls are boxed in (activity 2,3). Likewise the interior may not be finished (activity 4,6) until after the foundation is laid (activity 1,2), the walls are boxed in (activity

2,3), the floor is installed (activity 2,4), and the walls are closed in (activity 3,4). Arranging each of the activities in a network diagram clearly indicates to the manager the appropriate and necessary sequencing of the activities.

Perhaps the most important administrative use that can be made of such a network however is the determination of the "critical path." A path through any network is defined as a sequence of connected activities that leads from the beginning of the project (event 1) to the end of the project (event 6). Note carefully that all of the activities described in the network must be done before the project is considered complete, but that one of the paths through the network requires the most work, and this particular path is called the "critical path." The path is critical in the sense that if the manager wishes to reduce the time which the entire project will take, he must reduce the time of one or more of the activities along the critical path. It is also important because if any one or combination of the activities along the critical path takes more than the expected time listed in the network, the entire project will be delayed.

Finding the critical path in large PERT networks often requires an algorithm which is relatively easy to use. In this simple PERT network, however, we can use a "hit or miss" method in order to find the critical path. Keep in mind that the critical path is the longest path through this particular network. There are actually only three different paths through the small network in Table 17-3. The first path is signified by moving from event 1 to 2, 2 to 3, 3 to 5, and 5 to 6. The second path is signified by moving from event 1 to 2, 2 to 3, 3 to 4 and 4 to 6. And the final path is signified by moving from event 1 to 2, 2 to 4, and 4 to 6. The first of these paths would require 22 days to complete. This is calculated by adding together the activity times of those activities along the path.

Notice that activities along the path must be completed one after another and so it is appropriate to add the expected times for each of the activities in order to figure out the total amount of time that path would take to complete. In the case of the first path, we would add the activity lengths 4, 6, 4 and 8 together to arrive at the number 22. The second path would require us to add together the activity time 4, 6, 6 and 12 to arrive at 28. And the third path would require us to add together the activity times 4, 5 and 12 to arrive at 21.

The second of the paths in our particular PERT network, which runs from events 1 to 2, 2 to 3, 3 to 4, and 4 to 6, is the critical path, that is, it is the longest path through this PERT network. The number 28 tells us that this project will require *at least* 28 days for completion. There is no conceivable way (other than reducing some activity times) to complete this project in less than 28 days. Twenty-eight days is then referred to in PERT language as the "earliest completion time" for the project.

Each of those activities along the critical path, activity 1,2, activity 2,3, activity 3,4, and activity 4,6, is especially important to the administrator. It is these activities which if delayed will delay the entire project. Note that those activities which are not on the critical path, activity 2,4 for instance, if delayed, will not cause the entire project to be delayed. Activity 2,4 for instance could take six days rather than the expected five days, and the project could still be completed in 28 days. Each of the activities which is not on the critical path is referred to as having "slack time." Slack time is the extra time each of these activities could take without delaying the project. Note that those activites on the critical path have 0 slack time, that is, if any of them take longer than their expected times the entire project would be delayed. The identification of the critical path as those activities which the manager should pay the most attention to is a powerful planning technique.

PERT analysis should not be considered a stagnant process for drawing networks and calculating critical paths; it is actually a dynamic process which invites change and readjustment.

When there are changes in schedules or revisions of plans, in light of changing conditions, a PERT network allows the integration of these and supplies the administrator with information on the effects of these changes. The basic framework for PERT as explained above is a closed system network of activities and events that represent a project from its inception to its completion. The network which we used above depicted events and activities in their chronological sequences and in their explicit inter-relationships as conceived and scheduled by the project manager. This standard PERT approach often does not adequately cope with the uncertainty and instability associated with real world estimates of activity times and the resulting calculation of project completion time. For example, in the PERT analysis above activity 3,4 (closing in the walls) was estimeated to take six days. In the real world a great deal of uncertainty surrounds activity duration time, and the estimate of six days might not be realized when the project is actually begun.

The activity time, however, will usually vary over some range, and dependent upon where the actual activity time is within this range it may have an effect on the entire network of inter-related activities, even to the extent of completely changing the critical path configuration. Each activity and each activity time in the network may have such a potential effect.

In a very large and complex PERT network with several paths having roughly equal duration times, the probability of the critical path shifting to some other path is quite high. The actual critical path might possibly swing back and forth between several paths during the actual project. For example, activities along the critical path could take less time than anticipated and those of another path more than anticipated. It is often useful to know how the critical path might shift during the course of the project when the manager is in the planning stage. PERT analysis, as used in the field, is then often converted into a dynamic process by manipulating the network to predict how the real system might behave. Trials are often run on the PERT network using activity times that the manager considers to be possible and likely. By running many such trials the manager receives a useful indication of the degree of attention he should pay to each activity.

The models used in PERT analysis and those used in linear programming are called by operations researchers *deterministic* models; they are used when all the data and the relationships in the models are known with certainty. It is often the case, of course, that in the real world those conditions of certainty are not met, but it is also often the case that the real world situation is so minor a deviation from the assumption of certainty that the decision results arrived at through linear programming and PERT are quite useful to not-for-profit managers. In many cases, however, the environment in which the administrator of a not-for-profit firm operates is not certain. The method for dealing with uncertainty is to use probabilistic models. Probabilistic models assume that the values of the variables are not all known with certainty but that the manager knows more or less the various values that the variables may take. The final two planning techniques we will discuss, decision theory and simulation, are both examples of probabilistic models.

Decision Theory

Decision analysis is a form of planning and decision making used when decisions must be made sequentially and where uncertainty is an essential element of the situation. A decision theory model is as much like a roadmap as a linear programming model or a PERT model. The essential feature dealt with in a decision theory model, however, is its emphasis on the uncertainty of future situations as seen by the manager. Recall that all models are abstractions in which only certain elements are emphasized. In linear programming we emphasized competing uses for scarce resources. In PERT analysis the emphasis was on the inter-relationships between activities in a project and on the times that those activities required for completion. In decision theory the emphasis clearly rests on the uncertainty of outcome given various alternatives confronting the manager.

Most situations in which administrators would use decision theory are rather complicated because they tend to be long sequences of decisions with numerous uncertainties. The essentials of decision theory, however, can be outlined with a simple but realistic example of a single decision facing a manager where uncertainty is the key element in making the decision.

"Meals on Wheels" is a program designed to provide the elderly with meals at their homes three times a week. Elderly people in the city, if they desire a meal delivered to their home that evening, telephone the Meals on Wheels office by 3:00 in the afternoon and request the service. The meals are delivered in a truck with a heated insulated compartment much like a pizza delivery truck.

The meals are provided to the elderly at a charge of $1.00 per meal. These meals would normally cost an individual $3.00 on the average to prepare at home. The preparation cost to the "Meals on Wheels" program, however, is only $2.00 because of economies of large scale purchase and preparation. The administrator of the "Meals on Wheels" program faces an uncertain situation when deciding how many meals to prepare for a given day. Preparation of the meals must begin early in the morning. Meals which are prepared and not delivered are wasted. In order to ensure the good will of the elderly it is also a policy of the "Meals on Wheels" program to pay each of the elderly $3.00 in cash if the program is unable to provide a prepared meal on request.

The administrator in the example does know, however, that the number of calls received in the past has been somewhere between 50 and 70. It appears to the manager that there is an equal probability of receiving either 50, 60 or 70 calls on a given day. That is, about one-third of the time 50 calls are received by the "Meals on Wheels" program. One-third of the time 60 calls are received, and one-third of the time 70 calls are received. The administrator does not feel that there is any accurate way to predict the number of calls that will be received on any particular day.

The administrator's decision, then, is how many meals to produce on a given day such that he minimizes his expenses yet provides meals for as many callers as possible. The administrator may decide to use the most common form of decision theory which is a decision tree, presented in Table 17-4. Decision trees are normally drawn with standard symbols, and the accompanying diagram represents a simple decision tree for making the choice of whether to provide 50, 60 or 70 meals on a given day. The square node symbolizes the decision point. For each of the three alternatives open to the administrator it is standard practice to show a circular node from which branches emanate representing the possible outcomes which could result from the selection of this particular alternative. In the "Meals on Wheels" example, the decision facing the administrator is to provide 50, 60 or 70 meals, and so the square decision node has three branches emanating from it, one for each of these decisions. Following the topmost branch, which represents the decision of providing 50 meals, a numbered node in a circle branches out to indicate the three outcomes possible if the manager were to decide to provide the 50 meals.

Table 17-4   MEALS ON WHEELS: An Example of Decision Theory

—Each elderly person pays $1.00 for a meal which would cost $3.00 to prepare at
  home.
—Each meal costs "Meals on Wheels" $2.00 to prepare because of economics of large
  scale purchase and preparation.
—Meals not eaten go to waste.
—"Meals on Wheels" pays each person $3.00 cash if unable to deliver a prepared
  meal.

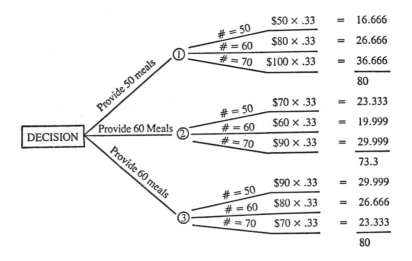

Provide 50 meals ①	# = 50	$50 × .33	=	16.666
	# = 60	$80 × .33	=	26.666
	# = 70	$100 × .33	=	36.666
				80
Provide 60 Meals ②	# = 50	$70 × .33	=	23.333
	# = 60	$60 × .33	=	19.999
	# = 70	$90 × .33	=	29.999
				73.3
Provide 60 meals ③	# = 50	$90 × .33	=	29.999
	# = 60	$80 × .33	=	26.666
	# = 70	$70 × .33	=	23.333
				80

DECISION

Assume: Probability of demand = 50 is 33⅓%
          Probability of demand = 60 is 33⅓%
          Probability of demand = 70 is 33⅓%

The circular node is often called a state of nature node. The
branch of the tree which becomes relevant after this node is not
dependent upon the choice which the manager makes but rather
is dependent upon how events over which the manager has no
control take place. We have already determined that regardless
of how many meals the manager decides to provide there is an

equal probability of either 50, 60 or 70 individuals calling the program for meal delivery. It is common practice at the end of each of the branches to list the outcome value for that particular branch.

In the case of the topmost branch the outcome would be $50.00. That is, the cost of the program of providing 50 meals and having just exactly 50 people call for meals on that particular day would bc $50.00 (providing 50 meals at $2.00 apiece would cost the program $100.00, but the program would also be paid $1.00 by each of the 50 individuals purchasing the meals, hence the total unreinbursed cost of the program would be $50.00). The second branch under the alternative to provide 50 meals lists an outcome value of $80.00, and the third outcome possible, if the administrator decides to provide 50 meals, would be a cost of $110.00. Since each of these outcomes is equally probable, given that the administrator decides to provide 50 meals, it is possible to calculate what statisticians call the expected value of the decision ''to provide 50 meals.''

The expected value of any variable is calculated by multiplying each of the outcomes by its expected probability and then summing these values. In this particular case, to calculate the expected value of the decision ''to provide 50 meals,'' we would multiply the first outcome, $50.00, by its expected probability, 33-⅓%. This figure would then be added to the second outcome, $80.00, multiplied by its respective probability, again 33-⅓%. That total would then be added to the third outcome multiplied by its expected probability. The calculations in the table show that the expected value of the alternative ''to provide 50 meals'' is $80.00. What the expected value means is that if the program continued to provide 50 meals over a very long period of time, and if the probability of calls were to remain as hypothesized, the average cost to the program on a per day basis would be $80.00 (the cheapest decision is shown in Table 17-4 to be providing 60 meals with an expected cost of $73.30).

What the decision tree has done for the administrator is merely to arrange the information which he has available in an order in which he can use it rationally. The decision tree, like the linear program or PERT analysis, does not make a decision for the administrator, but emphasizes the important aspects of a particular situation. The decision tree outlined above enjoys at least two important advantages. First, it structures the planning process, allowing the manager to approach decision making in an orderly and rational fashion, and secondly it forces the manager to examine all of the possible outcomes to his plan, both desirable and undesirable.

Simulation

Like decision theory, simulation models are probabilistic models. A simulation model imitates or mimics the behavior and the characteristics of a process or a system in which the manager is interested. Simulation is usually used by administrators of not-for-profit firms in those situations where experimenting or observing the actual process would be either too costly or too time consuming. The manager, therefore, reverts to describing a system as a mathematical model, or simulation, with trial data.

In many cases where administrators use simulation, it is not possible to develop a mathematical solution. There may exist within the organization mutually exclusive goals. In such a case, a simulation will be used to outline the alternatives.

Picture an archer aiming an arrow at a target approximately 100 yards away. The target is relatively small, and even though the archer is an experienced and proficient athlete, it is difficult to hit the target. Let's say that you desire to know the probability that an *even* number of hits occurs in ten shots of the arrow. In this situation it would be relatively easy to perform an experiment where the individual actually shot ten arrows at the target after which we could count the number of hits and identify whether that is an even number. In this simple case it is also possible mathematically to determine the probability of an even number of hits if we knew the probability that any particular shot would result in a hit. But we could also answer the question by reducing the situation to a simulation. While this particular situation is not difficult, or time consuming, or expensive to actually experiment with, it will provide a vehicle for explaining a simulation.

How will it be determined within the model whether a given simulated shot of the arrow hits the target or not? Picture a line with infinitely many points between 0 and 1. We many divide this line segment into two intervals between 0 and 1. One such interval could be 20% of the distance between 0 and 1, and the remainder would be the interval which would account for 80% of the distance between 0 and 1. Now if we knew the archer could hit the target 20% of the time and we wish to simulate a single shot of the arrow, we could draw a random number (from a random number generator or from a random number table) and check to see if that number fell within the 20% of the region between 0 and 1 which we might designate as "hit," or the 80% of the region between 0 and 1 which we might designate as "miss."

Let's assume that we divide the interval into two subsets. One subset will be the interval from 0 to .20000 inclusive. The other interval will begin just to the right of .2 and include the entire line segment up to the value of 1. By generating any random number now, and comparing it with these two intervals to find out if the simulated shot is a hit or a miss, we may easily simulate ten shots at the target. Ten simulated shots are listed in the accompanying table. Recall that any numbers generated between 0 and .2 inclusive are to be assigned to the "hit" category, while other numbers are to be assigned to the "miss" category. Of this particular set of ten shots nine were misses while only one was a hit. Now the reader can easily see that if the simulation were repeated again and again over many hundreds of times that the percentage of hits would be about 20%. In a given simulation run, however, like the one in the table, it is quite possible to have more than 20% of the shots resulting in hits or less than 20% of the shots resulting in hits.

Table 17-5   Archery Simulation

hit   miss

0	.2		1

Random Numbers Generated	Represents
.50979	miss
.61237	miss
.02078	hit
.65395	miss
.34319	miss
.41152	miss
.78425	miss
.3427	miss
.64886	miss

To answer our original question, in how many cases would there be an even number of hits among the ten shots, we would merely count the number of instances which we had simulated in which that happens. Then we would divide that number by the number of simulation runs we had calculated. The resulting probability, given that we had performed many simulation runs, would be very, very close to the number that we would arrive at by having the archer perform the experiment many times. Recall that the value of simulation lies in the fact that it can be used in those cases where it is impossible because of the magnitude of difficulty to calculate a deterministic answer, and in those cases where it would be difficult to actually perform the experiment because of expense or time delay.

An example of the real world use of simulation occurred a number of years ago when the New York Fire Department

analyzed the deployment of its fire boats in New York Harbor.[6]
In 1965 the City of New York had nine fire boats located at nine
different marine terminals around the New York Harbor. The
researchers wished to determine if a new deployment of less
than 9 fire boats could allow a single fire boat to reach any
incident in the harbor within six minutes. They wished also to
run a second simulation which would test the feasibility of a
single fire boat reaching any incident within twelve minutes.
The reason the time was so important in a simulation of fire
boats was that the managers considered that the sooner a fire
boat arrived at an incident the more quickly a fire could be
brought under control and thus the less damage would actually
be done. A particular response time then became the objective of
the manager.

Data was collected on the number of times the fire boats were
needed in the years 1965, 1966 and 1967, on where they were
needed and on what particular dates and times they were needed.
Each of these incidents of fire were plotted on a map of the
New York City Harbor. Four alternative location plans for
deploying the fire boats were actually simulated. Note that the
managers could have obtained the same data by actually making
these new deployments of fire boats and then allowing an
interval of time, say a year, for observation. As a means of
finding the best of the four deployments, this could be a rather
expensive and time consuming process.

Four alternative deployments of fire boats were selected for
analysis. They used less than the 9 boats currently employed.
The result of the simulations showed that the number of cases in
which the response time would be longer than six minutes was
exceedingly small. Thus the manager selected what he considered to be the best of the "innovative" deployments and
suggested it to the city as a means of conserving on resources

[6]For a synopsis of the original study done by R. Feeley of the Budget Bureau of the City
of New York, see *Systematic Analysis* by Harley Hinrichs and Graeme Taylor, pp.
83-91.

while maintaining roughly the same fire protection available with the entire nine boats.

While almost any simulation may be carried out manually, simulations today are almost always done on a computer. Computers are ideally suited to performing the iterative calculations required in a simulation. Just as in the case of linear programming, there are a number of special purpose simulation packages and languages which allow an administrator with little knowledge of the computer to run rather complicated simulations. The most common of these special purpose packages is the General Purpose System Simulator (GPSS). GPSS was developed and is maintained by IBM for most of its computer systems. Little or no computer programming knowledge is required for GPSS.

18

ACCOUNTABILITY: HOW TO GET MOVING

... IN THE RIGHT DIRECTION

Can not-for-profit firms be well managed? To ask the question is to indicate that there is a problem unique to such firms. Good management in a profit-seeking firm is measured in terms of profit or loss, but this has no bearing on good management in not-for-profit organizations. Perhaps the fundamental aspect of the problem has been the lack of *any* type of precise analysis and its application to not-for-profit firms, or of assuming that the nature of not-for-profit organizations precludes establishment of effective guidelines.

Benefit-cost analysis, for example, is essentially an *ex ante* concept, which means that it attempts to evaluate a project *before* it is undertaken or determine whether it should be undertaken. In practice, however, benefit-cost analysis does not really determine what goods and services will be provided by not-for-profit firms. Rather, custom, the strength of pressure groups and public-choice determine what will be supplied.

Evolving from the social choice process, a certain not-for-profit firm will be established to provide a particular good or service. The primary purpose of this chapter is to examine the mandate given the particular not-for-profit firm and the means available to carry out the mandate. Whether alternative projects might be worthy or have a higher probability of success is, therefore, outside the scope of this analysis.

The Lack of Precise Objectives: Shooting in the Dark

The administrator of a not-for-profit firm is often confronted with a fuzzy statement about what to do, given a budget, seldom or never told precisely what is to be done, how it should be done, or what means will be used to check performance. Such organizations, of course, have little difficulty in hiring administrators to head them! The most effective institutions, however, attempt to precisely state what they are doing and have clear objectives known by all who finance, sponsor, review, are serviced by, and who work at such agencies.

Consider the objectives of universities (typically not-for-profit firms) in the United States. Most universities in the nineteenth century in the United States were either church-related schools (e.g. Harvard, Dartmouth, Antioch and Lehigh) or were elitist liberal institutions (e.g. Columbia, William and Mary, Northwestern, Vanderbilt and Stanford). The church-related schools, unlike most modern universities, had clearly defined objectives: to educate young men and women for careers in the clergy or to prepare them to lead "moral" lives as outlined by the religious beliefs of a particular organized religion. The elitist liberal universities were also goal-directed: these institutions were designed for training the children of the well-to-do in the humane arts.

In both types of early American universities the administrators and the lower level managers (i.e. the faculty) had few questions about who ran the university; there was little pressure for different forms of university organization. The control of both types of universities rested squarely with those who contributed the money to run the institutions, and those same individuals set the goals of providing religious education and/or training in the humanities.

A commercial restaurant, on the other hand, provides a service, sometimes well and sometimes poorly; but it is not essential for the profit-seeking restaurant to define precisely what that service means: nutritious food or cheap food, friendly or formal atmosphere, pleasant employees or unobtrusive catering. The profit and loss statement and the continuing survival of the restaurant will indicate whether the proper trade-offs are being made between what constitutes a well-run restaurant or one poorly run.

What is the appropriate standard against which a not-for-profit firm should be evaluated? How does one measure success when there are multiple objectives? Conflicting objectives? Intangible and nonquantifiable objectives? Some suggest that standards for not-for-profit firms are unnecessary. After all, they reason, not-for-profit firms are run by professionals who know their business and are of high professional caliber. These individuals know what is best for their constituents and sponsors and will provide these goods and services with absolute integrity.

At the risk of offending omniscient professionals we dare to suggest that some guidelines for measuring the output of not-for-profit firms be specified; to suggest further, that clarity in specifying the objectives of a not-for-profit institution is critical. Once the objectives are specified, the struggle to agree upon evaluation criteria, including some measurement of output, begins.

At least three points must be made about the evaluation process in general:

1. Ideally, the evaluation mechanism should be developed as the firm is established; the search for a process of evaluation should be part of the search for objectives.
2. It is essential to distinguish between two types of evaluation processes: the measurement of output of the firm and the extent to which it is doing that which it was set up to do; and the measurement of the extent to which its operations reflect the moral constraints specified by the sponsor.

3.   Internal evaluations are helpful but seldom accurate. Internal data systems are often biased justification for the firm's survival or expansion, used as proof of demand, which, given the subsidies many not-for-profit firms receive, may be very misleading. Whenever possible an adversary approach to evaluation is more desirable.

Whether internal or external checks are chosen, the central problem is still one of finding adequate measures of output for a not-for-profit firm. The relationship between the final objective, which often cannot be measured, and some intermediate variable becomes critically important. Because the end product itself often cannot be quantitatively defined, proxies must be monitored. We refer to these proxies as targets and indicators.

Targets and Indicators

The indicator-operational target approach is a pragmatic method of improving the performance of a not-for-profit firm. It originates in the assumption that no one has complete information about the way policy actions filter through the organization, are modified by other factors, and ultimately result in some type of output.

Policy-makers are concerned with two major questions when developing procedures for not-for-profit firms. Primarily, they want to know what effect the various actions of the not-for-profit firm will have on the overall objective. For example, what will be the effect of a government-backed mortgage program on the availability of housing? An *indicator* which is easily observed and can be closely watched, such as new housing starts, might provide information about the ultimate objective, availability of housing. Those responsible for policy also need to know how they should manipulate their support and control of the firm to ensure that the agency is exerting the desired efforts towards the ultimate objective. An *operational target* provides a method for ensuring that the desired effort level is met. In the case of a government-backed mortgage program, the interest rate on home mortgages could be an operational target.

An indicator is defined as a variable that provides information about the effect of current firm activity on future movements in the ultimate objectives. Empirical evidence in organizational theory confirms that the effect of actions on the ultimate objective is distributed over time. Hence, the firm's sponsor cannot accurately judge the effect of current policy actions on the ultimate objectives of the policy by looking directly at the ultimate objectives. Changes in the reading levels of senior high school students in a particular school district reflect, for example, actions taken in a previous period.

Sponsors do not need indicators to tell them the current intent of their own policy. They already know what they intend to accomplish with their programs. However, they do need information about the influence their past policies are exerting on the course of the ultimate objective.

The choice of an indicator involves selecting some variable that consistently provides reliable information about influences of present actions on the status of the ultimate objective. In general terms, this requires that a change in the magnitude of an indicator is followed by a predictable change in the magnitude of the ultimate objective of the policy. For example, expanding the amount of time in a curriculum on reading (i.e., the current policy) should gradually result in better performance on reading tests, which is the indicator, and finally in the better reading performance, the ultimate objective. The assumption is that reading test scores correlate well with better reading.

A variable that meets the indicator criterion can serve as a scale that permits sponsors to make meaningful statements about the relative effects of different policy actions on the ultimate policy objectives. It provides a means of relative comparison of different sets of policy actions, not necessarily an absolute means of comparison.

The usefulness of an indicator, let us repeat, hinges on whether or not it consistently supplies reliable information to the sponsors. If, at times, the ultimate policy objectives move in a direction opposite to that predicted by a given indicator, then the indicator has provided false information to the sponsor about the thrust of policy actions on the ultimate objectives.

An operational target is a separate and distinct concept from that of an indicator. *The operational target should satisfy three basic criteria:*

1. The sponsoring organization should be able to measure accurately the magnitude of the operational target shortly after a policy action is taken.
2. By manipulating the budget and other policy instruments, the sponsor should be able, in a very short period of time, to offset any other factors acting to change the magnitude of the operational target.
3. Changes in the magnitude of the operational target over an intermediate period of time should dominate changes in the magnitude of the variable chosen as an indicator.

Aren't operational targets and indicators much the same? Why does an administrator need a target if he already has a good indicator? The necessity for the introduction of operational targets, as in the case of indicators, arises basically from incompleteness of information. An indicator helps the sponsor to judge *the thrust* of policy influences on the future values of the ultimate objectives. An operational target helps the sponsor to *maximize control* over the intermediate movements of the indicator. In the case of improved reading skills, the operational target could be the actual number of hours spent on teaching reading at each grade level.

The implementation problem may be diagrammed. The extent of a sponsor's direct control is illustrated by enclosing the part of the transmission mechanism under its direct control—policy instruments—in a box. The elements of transmission lying wholly within the control of the not-for-profit firm consist of policy instruments and operational targets. In a reading program, these are resources and policy. The indicators are located as the connecting link between the not-for-profit firms and the ultimate objectives of the policy, which lie in the real world. The real world, in the reading example, consists of all those things over which the sponsor does not have control, for instance, the *ability* of the students to learn how to read, the *values* the students place on reading skills, and other socio-cultural conditions. However, implied in this methodology is the assumption that policy decisions by the sponsor will work through the system to provide results which may to some extent be controlled and accounted for.

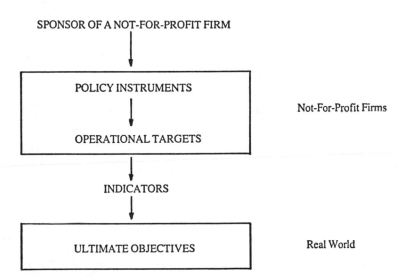

SPONSOR OF A NOT-FOR-PROFIT FIRM

POLICY INSTRUMENTS

Not-For-Profit Firms

OPERATIONAL TARGETS

INDICATORS

ULTIMATE OBJECTIVES

Real World

Targets and Indicators In Use

Recall that the use of targets and indicators is necessary in not-for-profit firms to make judgments on the effectiveness and the efficiency of the firm or the agency. Effectiveness is concerned with how well the not-for-profit firm does its job and is always related to the goals of the firm. Efficiency is a measure of output per unit of input, regardless of whether the output is related to the ultimate goals of the organization. Both effectiveness and efficiency must be considered when choosing targets and indicators.

The use of targets and indicators in not-for-profit agencies is probably best understood in the context of an actual situation. The United States Naval Supply Center located in Newport, Rhode Island, is one not-for-profit firm that has attempted to use specific targets and indicators to judge its effectiveness and efficiency.

Newport, Rhode Island, has been a deep water anchorage for men-of-war since 1694 when Robert Melville suggested its use as a Navy yard to the Royal Navy. The Naval Supply Center at Newport has as its principal mission to receive, store and issue material for its customers, the one-hundred and twenty-eight fleet units (ships and navy battalions) and one-hundred and sixty-seven naval shore facilities (including such operations as shipyards and aircraft overhaul facilities).

The annual operating budget for this supply facility in the early 1970s ran to just over seven million dollars per year. Over six-hundred people worked at the facility and forty-five thousand supply transactions were completed annually (i.e., 175 supply transactions per working day). The material supplied by the Center covered almost everything navy units could use from fuel and electronic repair parts to frozen meats; approximately fifty-thousand different items were carried in its inventory.

The management of each United States Naval Supply facility is required to furnish periodic reports to its Washington headquarters. These reports include the targets and indicators discussed below and have been used to evaluate the Newport center and to compare its performance with that of other Navy supply centers.

Four operational targets were used by the Newport Center in the early 1970s: (1) receipts, (2) issues, (3) shipments and (4) demands. Recall that operational targets ought to be readily measurable, ought to be under the control of the management of the supply facility, and ought to dominate any changes in the indicator or indicators. In short, operational targets should help the sponsor, in this case the Washington headquarters, to maximize its control over the supply facility.

Receipts were the measure in both line items and measurement tons of the material coming into the Newport Center. Washington suggested that the supply center should be able to process 85% of all its receipts within seven days. Processing means listing the receipts in stock records and storing the goods in a suitable location where they are ready for issue to the fleet.

Issues was the term used by the supply facility for its measure of whether or not items requested could be located and supplied. From time to time, a request for materials had to be denied because of improper record keeping or the storage of material in an inaccessible or inconvenient location. Washington set as an operational target the fulfillment of at least 99% of all requests.

Shipments were also measured in both line items and measurement tons. The target supplied by headquarters was to ship 95% of all requests within twelve days of the arrival of an order.

Demands were measured only in line items. These were customer requests acted upon by the Center (or referred to other Navy Supply Centers). Washington wished to view demand from the customer's point of view as gross availability; that is, the probability that a demand or request could be filled by the Center in a reasonable time period. The Center might not be able to fulfill a request because the Center's management had chosen not to stock such an item, replenishments of certain items were tardy, or the materials were ordered only when requests were entertained. The Washington headquarters set the availability objectives for inventory in terms of a percentage of requests received. Each of these operational targets were summarized by Washington and reported weekly to the United States Navy Supply Center management in Newport.

Because the objective of the organization was to provide service at minimum cost, the operational targets, which were largely output measures, were used in conjunction with cost indicators to determine operating efficiency. The Supply Center was divided into 50 responsibility centers, which were charged with measurable "costs" or expenses. In turn, each job order was charged "prices," uniquely identified with each entity within the organization. At the end of each month, a report was prepared indicating the budgeted and actual "costs" as well as the total value of the work completed by each responsibility center.

While the operating targets and indicators used by the United States Naval Supply Center were certainly not perfect proxies for efficiency and effectiveness, they did provide the management of this not-for-profit agency and its sponsoring organization (the Washington headquarters) with a number of measures which essentially acted as proxies for the all-inclusive profit measure used by profit-seeking corporations.

It is interesting to note that the Naval Supply Center at Newport attempted successfully to improve its performance, as measured by the operational targets and indicators, by introducing an innovation titled SERVMART. SERVMART reduced the problems of customers submitting requisitions.

Previously, many customers experienced costly delays, even though a priority system of requisitions moved fairly rapidly through the system. SERVMART was essentially a self-service facility for high usage items. Customers (Navy personnel assigned to ships, battalions or shore activities) merely selected in person the items needed and exited through a check-out counter much like a supermarket. Each ship battalion or shore activity was charged for the cost of material which it had "purchased." The savings to the center in handling and delivery costs and the decrease in processing time was extraordinary. Both the operational targets and indicators of the Naval Supply Center reflected this improved performance. The concept has now been widely adopted throughout the United States Navy.

A second example of the target indicator approach in a not-for-profit firm is provided by the Employment Development Department of the State of California. The Department has as its major objective to provide job placement to the unemployed and underemployed. The Department maintains over one-hundred offices in both large cities and small towns.

The sponsor of the department (i.e., the State of California government) wished to place special emphasis on certain groups of employment applicants such as veterans of the armed services, minorities, unemployment insurance claimants, handicapped individuals, etc. The department wished to give priority in placing these individuals as well as quality employment. As an operational target, the department chose to use a weighted average of the kinds of employment actually provided during a given peroid. A "score" was given to each local field office based on the number of placements in each of the various categories (i.e., veterans, minorities, handicapped, etc.). Heavier weights were assigned to those groups which the department wished to emphasize. Each placement officer and each placement office was assigned a score using what was referred to as the balance placement formula.

As a proxy for quality of employment, the Department decided on the length of time in the job as a reasonable indicator. Note that this variable which would provide information about the effect of current agency activity could only be measured at some point in time in the future. The "scores" of the various placement officers and offices were adjusted to reflect job duration after that information became available.

Regular reports were sent by each field office to the Department in order to provide information on performance among offices. Because of hesitancy in explicitly defining proxies for efficiency and effectiveness of the agency, the balance placement formula and its adjustment for job quality were implemented slowly. While other targets and indicators are undoubtedly used by the department, the implementation of this target and indicator significantly increased the control of the sponsoring agency, the state of California, over the Employment Development Department and its numerous local offices.

Kicking a Dead Horse

Getting a not-for-profit firm to do what it should may be compared to kicking a dead horse. The sponsor, administrator, and user seem powerless. On the other hand, some not-for-profit firms seem to be running off like untamed broncos. In both cases, the individuals in the firm are reacting to the incentives with which they are confronted.

In India, at one time, the operational target of the population control agency was the absolute number of sterilizations performed. In order to increase the seeming effectiveness of the firm, the administrators filled their tallies with old men and young boys who were easy to locate. This actually contributed little to the sponsor's ultimate objectives.

If public universities are funded based on the number of students enrolled in their classes as of a certain date (the operational target), the incentive is to pack the classrooms up to the given date. Quality surely suffers, virtually all who apply are accepted. Faculty who fail to cooperate in maintaining students in classes, at least until the "body count" date, are criticized by their superiors.

Likewise, if universities were to use student-written evaluations of faculty as the sole indicator for faculty promotion, salary, and tenure, the faculty would react. Exams would become "opportunities" for faculty to bribe students for good evaluations. (On the other hand, if only the "publish or perish" indicator were used, students would be neglected.) Employees in not-for-profit firms are like other individuals; they respond to incentives.

Precise objectives are essential for the effective delivery of goods and services in the not-for-profit sector. Because the output of a service agency often cannot be measured directly, proxies must be used. An indicator tests the effect of the actions of the service agency on the overall objective. A target provides a method for ensuring that the agency is exerting the desired effort level toward the ultimate objective. Those who choose to earn their living in not-for-profit firms respond to whatever is used to evaluate their performance. Hence, inappropriate indicators will yield undesirable outcomes.

19

ALTERNATIVES

"The wish is not always parent to the deed," lamented George Bernard Shaw, and nowhere is this more demonstrated than in not-for-profit firms. The most precise statement of objectives, the best techniques, and faultless indicators of performance will not guarantee delivery of the product unless the not-for-profit firm is set up to accomplish the stated goals. Depending on the particular not-for-profit firm under consideration, a search for alternatives which are unique, not to say outlandish, must be made to nudge the firm in the proper direction.

The alternatives presented in this chapter are basically of two types. The first set suggests changing the incentives of managers in not-for-profit agencies, and the second, changing the structure of the not-for-profit firm. Many of these alternatives are based on the work of two individuals, Gordon Tullock, author of *The Politics of Bureaucracy,* and William Niskanen, author of *Bureaucracy and Representative Government.*

Changing the Incentives of Administrators

Any incentive for adminstrators in not-for-profit firms should induce them to maximize not the total budget but the difference between the obtainable budget and the minimal total cost of the service. Such an incentive would reduce both the problem of inefficiency and the problem of over-supply that are characteristic of conventional not-for-profit firms.

Could the adminstrator be permitted to appropriate as his or her personal income all or some proportion of the difference between the approved budget and the actual cost? What would be the reaction if school superintendents were allowed to pay themselves a yearly bonus equal to 25% of the difference between the budget allocated to the school district and the district's costs? Or consider the case of the head administrator of a large metropolitan hospital being paid a yearly bonus to his/her salary equal to some percentage, perhaps 100% of the difference between the allocated budget and the total costs for the year. The acceptance of such proposals for incentive payments to administrators of public service agencies seems rather unlikely. However, it is a very realistic proposal for small private not-for-profit firms, such as credit unions, and it deserves serious consideration.

In spite of our pessimism about the widespread implementation of such an incentive system, it is instructive to ponder what its outcome would be. If an administrator operating under such a system did increase the "profits," best thought of as a residual, the school board or university board of directors would be provided with a much clearer picture of the level of service that *could* be provided for a given budget allocation. Recall that the budget review committee of a sponsor is often just searching in the dark for accurrate cost estimations.

Some would criticize such a system, arguing that the administrators would be confronted with an incentive system which could endanger the quality of the service provided. Would not the school superintendent or the university president, these critics ask, have an incentive to reduce costs by providing very poor service in order to be able to pocket the difference between the allocated budget and actual costs? It must be admitted that this is precisely what would happen if the particular not-for-profit firm had some sort of monopoly power. School districts and public universities certainly do have at least some monopoly power. But even where monopoly power exists, some services could be easily and cheaply spotchecked (using targets and indicators). The check would see if the level of services is being maintained. Such spot-checks would leave the administrator with the incentive to reduce costs while maintaining quality and quantity of service, which is precisely the desired outcome. Examples of not-for-profit firms which have easily measured output and hence might easily be organized under such a system are those responsible for processing welfare payments, tax returns, and the air traffic control agencies.

An additional criticism of the proposal suggests that such an incentive system would operate effectively for a very short period of time, perhaps a year. A program which operates efficiently for one year tends in practice to find the budget for the following year cut by the sponsor. Clearly, it is the case that the administrator will have to trade off gain in the present versus future gain. If, however, the administrator is competing with other agencies in the provision of a service, the budget review committee will have comparable data for what is an acceptable level of performance and the sponsor could quite reasonably use this to determine the budget allocation. It might be added that a sponsor which would consciously set out to penalize the efficient administrator by lowering his or her effective salary would probably receive precisely the type of perfomance it is willing to pay for!

As a final comment on this type of system, note that one of the weaknesses of the system might be turned into one of its greatest strengths. Sponsors could induce efficient managers to take over divisions that traditionally yield very low residuals by providing them with generous budget allocations. Once the managers had taken over these low residual divisions, the incentive system would work to induce the managers to transform the divisions into efficient operating units. Thus, by "over-budgeting" for a short period of time a sponsor could induce the most efficient managers to take what might seem at first glance the most unattractive of positions.

But why spend a great deal of time analyzing an incentive system that has a low likelihood of ever being introduced in most not-for-profit situations? While it is true that the exact system described above probably has a low likelihood of being introduced, variations of the same idea might be much more acceptable and could provide similar results. For example, administrators could be paid not only a salary during their tenure in office, but could be rewarded with deferred payments for unusually efficient administration. These deferred payments are similar to the portion of the premium the salesman of an insurance policy receives for the life of the policy as long as the premium is paid. It is very difficult to recognize the level and quality of output during an adminstrator's tenure in office. A system of deferred payments would preclude the administrator from causing the deterioration of the capital assets of the firm without regard to replacement. The manager of a credit union, in our previous example, could reduce maintenance on plant and equipment during his or her tenure in office, in order to reduce costs and thus increase his/her "bonus." However, the deterioration in the buildings and equipment of the credit union would become apparent after the manager's tenure in office. Because the payments under the second proposed system would be deferred, the manager could be penalized for his or her actions in allowing the deterioration of capital assets.

A second variation of our original incentive system would permit the administrator to spend some proportion of the difference between the approved budget and the actual cost on a restricted set of items. A not-for-profit firm would receive an approved budget and would be expected to perform a set of approved activities. Other activities which might contribute to morale within the firm would be allowed. These activities would be financed from the residual between the allocated budget and actual costs. An example of these "other activities" for a school superintendent could be plush rugs for the office, expensive paneling for his or her office suite, a generous travel budget for the superintendent and his or her staff, or a convention expenditure allowance. Under current review and audit procedures for not-for-profit firms, there is an unfortunate tendency for auditors and the more traditional budget review officers to eliminate the amentites, listed under "other activities," and thus penalize efficient administrators. This tendency to penalize efficient administrators would be eliminated by explicitly approving such *seemingly* frivolous and unproductive expenditures.

Changing the Structure of the Not-For-Profit Sector

When consideration is given to efficient provisions of services by not-for-profit firms, it is also important to examine the environment in which the not-for-profit firm is operating. While changes in the incentive systems for administrators can bring about changes in efficiency, changes in the structure of the not-for-profit sector may be more significant in bringing about desired results. The centerpiece of a plan for making not-for-profit firms more responsive to customers and sponsors would be an increase in competition among the firms that supply the same or similar services. In addition, changes in sponsor financing and the budget review process yield increases in efficiency.

As economic argument for monopoly supply by not-for-profit firms must be based on economies of scale; but large economies of scale justifying monopoly supply have seldom empirically been demonstrated in the real world. It is often argued, for example, that one and only one obstetrics department is needed in a town. This conclusion is based on the small number of births in a given town and the need to avoid "costly" duplication of services. It is argued further that one hospital could specialize in the type of equipment and staff needed to efficiently provide this service. These arguments commonly find their way into public forums, but they overlook the important fact that the wastes of monopolistic provision may counteract gains realized from competition. The obstetrics staff in the hospital, chosen to provide the monopoly service, will have less incentive to provide the quality of service necessary for survival in a competitive environment. Additionally, what incentive is there for the hospital to specialize in excellent neo-natal care, if they are guaranteed routine and problem deliveries without any particular effort on their part to achieve distinction and quality?

In general, not-for-profit firms have budget-maximizing incentives to broaden their service line. Oftentimes these firms provide new services which have little relation to those they were intended to produce. Nor is there any cost reason to produce the services jointly. Universities seem to have a tendency to offer a major in practically every field. Not-for-profit firms, in general, also have a budget-ensuring incentive to broaden their service line as a hedge against the uncertainties of demand and cost conditions for the original services. This incentive clearly leads to the production of services with significantly different demand and cost conditions. State teachers' colleges, for example, when confronted with graduates unable to get teaching positions because of over-supply, hastily expanded their offerings to avoid extinction. Note that most state teachers' colleges have evolved into full-line four-year public universities. There are "good" and "bad" aspects to this tendency. The "good" aspect is that the lack of specialization leads to competition between firms producing the same good or service. The "bad" aspect is that the good may be overproduced. The challenge for sponsors of not-for-profit firms is to use this natural competiton in the not-for-profit sector to generate an optimal supply of public services.

Competition among not-for-profit firms can be used to reduce the inefficiency characteristic of a monopoly firm in several ways. Any firm subject to competition finds that the customer is now in a position to take his business elsewhere. In essence, the demand for the service of the firm becomes more elastic. Faced with this demand, the agency has an incentive to seek out and use more efficient production processes. Hence, specialization may ensue from the competitive process.

An additional benefit accrues to society if the not-for-profit firm is subject to competition. Competition brings about two conditions which increase the probability that a sponsor reviewing the budget will be able to identify and approve a lower total budget for a given level of output. First, the sponsor will now have access to information from alternative firms on costs. Comparisons can be made between the given firm's stated costs and the alternative firm's costs. Administrators of competing obstetrical units in various hospitals, for example, will be anxious to point out to customers and sponsors wide variations in costs that cannot be explained by differences in the quality. Secondly, if a not-for-profit firm is placed in a position where it must compete for customers, it will be less likely to use factors of production which are strongly represented on the sponsor's budget review committee. For example, if a school district must minimize costs, it is less likely to specify musical instruments in such a way that only the company owned by a school board member could supply them. The administrators will realize that their costs will be compared with the costs of their competitors. If the given school's costs are out of line, the sponsoring agency will become suspect and may, perhaps, reduce its budget vindictively.

The most desirable effect of competing not-for-profit firms from a social point of view is the greater diversity that would result from the production process. Differentiated service from several firms would, over time, improve and maintain quality in a way that a monopoly franchise never would. Hence, new not-for-profit firms should be encouraged, and old ones permitted to expire. There must be free entry into and free exit out of the market in order for there to be a truly competitive environment. This does not mean that at any one point in time there must be more than one firm providing a particular service; but it does mean that at any point in time, there must be the possibility that new firms may enter the field and that old firms be eliminated by their sponsors. Basically, we are suggesting that not-for-profit firms be forced to compete in a way that anti-trust laws encourage profit-seeking firms to compete. Unfortunately, the environment in which not-for-profit firms operate is one where the conventional wisdom is an explicit, consistent, and enforced policy against competition and duplication.

Recall that all goods and services provided for collectively need not be produced in the not-for-profit sector! A community or club which decides to subsidize the consumption of a good by its members need not produce the good. Private profit-seeking or not-for-profit firms can bid to supply certain services. In the United States most buildings used by government agencies are constructed by private firms; most military equipment and supplies are developed and produced by private firms, and the food services in many government buildings and military bases are supplied by private firms. Many more services could be contracted out, however. Private firms could conceivably bid to manage the postal service, fire protection, air traffic control, and even police protection.

Finally, many not-for-profit firms have carefully cultivated ties with individuals on budget review committees (the sponsors). An adversary relationship between the budget review committee and the administrators of the agency providing the service would certainly reduce costs and increase the quality and quantity of services provided.

To provide this adversary relationship we would suggest a random assignment and periodic reassignment of individuals to the directing boards or review committees. This would certainly be better than the counterproductive long tenures of board members which we observe in practice.

20

CONCLUSION

University education, when examined through economist's eyes, assumes characteristics of a unique industry. This is because; (1) those who consume its produce do not purchase it; (2) those who produce it do not sell it; and (3) those who finance it do not control it.[1]

Change "university education" to "the not-for-profit firm" and the above quotation remains a valid statement. Consequently, not-for-profit institutions have remained outside the mainstream of microeconomic theory. To even suggest that these institutions be questioned about their effectiveness and efficiency horrifies those who work within them.

The reaction is legitimate. Not-for-profit firms are producing a "process, a happening through time, to which the (user) submits in the knowledge that he will become and remain sensorily different from what he is. The genuine . . . process 'transforms.' It does this not suddenly but over a time constrained sequence . . . Prospective customers find themselves in a curious stiuation of committing themselves in favor of a product they do not know. (It) is like a blind date."[2]

Good nursing, for example, has little to do with organization and high technology. Rather, nursing at its best is able to bring

[1] J.M. Buchanan and N. E. Devletoglou, *Academia in Anarchy: An Economic Diagnosis* (New York: Basic Books, 1970), p.8.

[2] Ibid, pp. 12-13.

patients around the bend when the patients themselves seem to have lost the will and/or strength to recover. Good educational institutions do something quite similar for their students. Success in either of these processes, however, is not guaranteed. Consequently, there is much talk about the need for "good people" in not-for-profit firms. Presumably, "good people" refers to intelligent, well-trained individuals with great moral character; of course, if they also have leadership ability, that is an asset! The main thesis of this book, however, is that merely increasing the presence of these people, if indeed this could be accomplished, would not necessarily improve the effectiveness of government, in particular, and the not-for-profit sector in general. One who has lived in an economically under-developed area is perhaps best able to appreciate how futile are the efforts of the finest individuals when the set of institutional arrangements in which they labor is not conducive to productivity.

The goal of a not-for-profit firm should be to provide the framework in which "ordinary" individuals provide the intended good or service reasonably effectively and efficiently. Such a not-for-profit firm would, of course, not squander, but rather employ, the scarce and valuable resources embodied in the intelligence, training and moral character of individuals within the firm. It hardly seems necessary, but perhaps it is useful to emphasize that not-for-profit firms, public and private, must enforce the minimum legal and behavioral code under which they choose to operate.

Discussions of efficiency and effectiveness in economic theory generally focus on the entrepreneur, the capitalist, and the consumer each attempting to force the organizaton to operate on its behalf. Even discussion of productivity in Socialist economic organization hinges on a system that has at least one exogenous variable, namely central direction. Seldom are efficiency and effectiveness discussed in terms of explicit cooperation among individuals.[3] However, communal or collective ownership-consumption arrangements, namely not-for-profit firms, dominate such areas as health care, education, and even financial institutions. Historical accident, rather than any public good criteria, explains the origin of many not-for-profit societies which exist today. Over a long period of time, many have performed needed economic services. Yet, the theory of the profit-seeking firm, even when the customer is paying full marginal cost, fails to explain the outcomes of firms which operate under the legal, traditional and motivational characteristics of their not-for-profit heritage.[4]

Must one then presume that not-for-profit firms cannot be reasonably efficient and effective? No, because, in the case of a public good, they produce what otherwise could not be produced in the market, and, in the short run, may be used to challenge a profit-seeking monopoly. Often, such a firm materially and spiritually improves the condition of its constituencies.

However, there are some necessary conditions that must hold or the not-for-profit firm will exist only by virtue of the subsidy it receives from its sponsor or by virtue of its tax-exempt status. These conditions require first of all vigilance by someone or some group in setting and monitoring the goals of the firm. Also, effectiveness and efficiency are best served when those in the organization agree to operate under the same code of behavior or have the same world view. Constant interchange of thought, experience and criticism, and the recognized possibility of substantial benefits from cooperation, may substitute for homogeneity. Optimal size of the organizaton (neither too large or too

---

[3]J. M. Buchanan, "An Economic Theory of Clubs," *Economica*, XXXII, (Feb., 1965), pp. 1-14.

[4]J. T. Croteau and R. A. Taylor, "The Economics of the Non-Profit Firm," a paper presented at the Meeting of the Atlantic Economic Association, Washington, D.C., October, 1975.

small) must be determined by the nature of what is produced. The firm must be able to exclude (or coerce) free riders. Finally, since competing institutions may retard institutional entropy, competition may even need to be created where it does not exist—competition not only between not-for-profit firms and their profit-seeking counterparts but also among not-for-profit firms. Finally, a not-for-profit firm, to be effective, must not attempt everything in its field and must struggle against the "need" to be cosmic in solving all the problems of mankind.

REFERENCES

Chapter 2

William Niskanen. *Bureaucracy and Representative Government,* Aldine Publishing Company, Chicago, 1971.

Robert Kaufman. *Are Government Organizations Immortal?* The Brookings Institution, Washington, D.C., 1976.

Thomas E. Copeland and Keith V. Smith. "An Overview of Nonprofit Organizations," *Journal of Economics and Business,* Volume 30 (2), 1978.

Chapter 3

Felix A. Nigro and Lloyd G. Nigro. *Modern Public Administration,* Fourth Edition, Harper & Row, New York, 1977.

Burton A. Weisbrod. *The Voluntary Nonprofit Sector,* Lexington Books, Lexington, Massachusetts, 1977.

Chapter 4

Vincent Ostrom. *The Intellectual Crisis in American Public Administration,* Revised Edition, The University of Alabama Press, University, Alabama, 1974.

Charles Wolf. "A Theory of Nonmarket Failure: Framework for Implementation Analysis," *Journal of Law & Economics.* Volume 22 (2), 1979.

Chapter 5

Gordon Tullock. *The Politics of Bureaucracy,* Public Affairs Press, Washington, D.C., 1965.

Joseph A. Uveges. *The Dimensions of Public Administration,* Second Edition, Holbrook Press, Boston, 1975.

James M. Buchanan. *The Limits of Liberty,* University of Chicago Press, Chicago, 1975.

Chapter 6

Oliver Williamson. *The Economics of Discretionary Behavior: Managerial Objectives in a Theory of the Firm,* Prentice-Hall, Englewood Cliffs, N.J., 1964.

Chapter 7

Gordon Tullock. *The Politics of Bureaucracy*, Public Affairs Press, Washington, D.C., 1965.

Chapter 8

James M. Buchanan and Marilyn R. Flowers, *The Public Finances: An Introductory Textbook*, Fourth Edition, Richard D. Irwin, Inc., Homewood, Illinois, 1975.

James M. Buchanan and Gordon Tullock, *The Calculus of Consent*, University of Michigan Press, Ann Arbor, MI., 1962.

Kenneth J. Arrow. *The Limits of Organization*, W. W. Norton, New York, 1974.

James M. Buchanan. *The Demand and Supply of Public Goods*, Rand McNally and Company, Chicago, 1968.

Chapter 9

Barry P. Keating. "The Characteristics and Survival of Public Interest Groups," *Atlantic Economic Journal*, Volume 5, Number 3, December, 1977.

Chapter 11

William Niskanen. *Bureaucracy and Representative Government*, Aldine Publishing Company, Chicago, 1971.

Chapter 12

William Niskanen. *Bureaucracy and Representative Government*, Aldine Publishing Company, Chicago, 1971.

Ludwig von Mises. *Bureaucracy*, Arlington House, New Rochelle, N.Y., 1969.

Barry P. Keating and Dolores Tremewan Martin. *Cases and Problems in Political Economy*, McGraw-Hill, New York, 1978.

Chapter 13

Bruce F. Davie and Bruce F. Duncombe. *Public Finance*, Holt, Rinehart and Winston, Inc., New York, 1972.

Barbara A. Gutek. "Strategies for Studying Client Statisfaction," *The Journal of Social Issues*, Volume 34, Number 4, 1978.

Chapter 14

Barry P. Keating. "The Rhetoric of Collective Bargaining in Universities," *Journal of collective Negotiations in the Public Sector*, Volume 4 (4), 1975.

Jack Stieber. *Public Employee Unionism*, Studies of Unionism in Government, The Brookings Institution, 1973.

Chapter 15

Emerson O. Henke. *Accounting for Nonprofit Organizations*, Wadsworth, Inc., Belmont, CA., 1966.

Chapter 16 and Chapter 17

Edith Stokey and Richard Zeckhauser. *A Primer for Policy Analysis*, W. W. Norton, New York, 1978.

Lester Bittel, Editor. *Encyclopedia of Professional Management*, McGraw-Hill, New York, 1978.

Richard Levin and Charles Kirkpatrick. *Quantitative Approach to Management*, McGraw-Hill, New York, 1978.

John Dinkel, Gary Kochenberger and Donald Plane. *Management Science*, Richard D. Irwin, Inc., Homewood, IL., 1978.

Chapter 18

Albert E. Berger. *The Money Supply Process*, Wadsworth, Inc., Belmont, California, 1971.

Chapter 19

William Niskanen. *Bureaucracy and Representative Government*, Aldine Publishing Company, Chicago, 1971.

Gordon Tullock. *The Politics of Bureaucracy*, Public Affairs Press, Washington, D.C., 1965.

Anthony Downs. *Inside Bureaucracy*, Little Brown and Company, Boston, 1967.

INDEX